THE
BIG
BOOK
OF
PALEO
PRESSURE
COOKING

THE BIG BOOK OF PALEO PRESSURE COOKING

150 Fast-to-Fix, Super-Delicious Recipes for All Brands of Electric Pressure Cookers, Including the Instant Pot

HARVARD COMMON PRESS

NATALIE PERRY

Inspiring | Educating | Creating | Entertaining

Brimming with creative inspiration, how-to projects, and useful information to enrich your everyday life, Quarto Knows is a favorite destination for those pursuing their interests and passions. Visit our site and dig deeper with our books into your area of interest: Quarto Creates, Quarto Cooks, Quarto Homes, Quarto Lives, Quarto Drives, Quarto Explores, Quarto Gifts, or Quarto Kids.

First Published in 2019 by The Harvard Common Press,
an imprint of The Quarto Group,
100 Cummings Center, Suite 265-D, Beverly, MA 01915, USA.
T (978) 282-9590 F (978) 283-2742 QuartoKnows.com

The Harvard Common Press titles are also available at discount for retail, wholesale, promotional, and bulk purchase. For details, contact the Special Sales Manager by email at specialsales@quarto.com or by mail at The Quarto Group, Attn: Special Sales Manager, 100 Cummings Center, Suite 265-D, Beverly, MA 01915, USA.

23 22 21 20 19   1 2 3 4 5

ISBN 978-1-55832-940-9

Digital edition published in 2019
eISBN 978-1-55832-941-6

Library of Congress Cataloging-in-Publication Data is available

Design and page layout: Laura McFadden Design, Inc.
Photography: Natalie Perry

Printed in China

To my four children,
who always ask for dinner to be done sooner.
With more bacon.

CONTENTS

Introduction: Paleo Under Pressure

"It's like a slow cooker and a microwave had a baby," is a response I often give when someone asks me what an Instant Pot is. It's the best way I can explain how you can have tender, slow-cooked meat and simmered sauces in lightning-fast time.

The wildly popular Instant Pot is a "multicooker," which means it can cook by more than one method. However, it is popular mainly for its fast-to-the-table capabilities as an electric pressure cooker, and most of the recipes we see for the Instant Pot are, in fact, pressure-cooking recipes. The recipes in this book are just such recipes. They also work in other models of electric pressure cookers and multicookers besides the Instant Pot. All of these makes and models of electric pressure cookers, both the Instant Pot and its cousins, are gaining popularity and making it even easier to get delicious meals on the table fast.

The only thing better than a quick dinner is a quick, healthy dinner. That's where I come in. This cookbook is a collection of paleo-friendly recipes that you and your family will love. Paleo means free of grains (and gluten), dairy, legumes, and refined sugar. Recipes like Buffalo Ranch Chicken Chowder (page 67) and Green Chile Shredded Beef (page 102) will become part of your dinner rotation. And don't forget about dessert—easy Peppermint Pots de Crème (page 218) will be a perfectly sweet ending to a weeknight meal.

You don't have to be a strict paleo follower to get the most out of this book, though. Those with food allergies or intolerances will benefit from gluten- and dairy-free recipes made from whole foods, and there are dozens of recipes that are also free from eggs and nuts.

Basically, electric pressure cookers have been life-changing for people who are striving for a healthy lifestyle and longing for cozy, home-cooked meals, but who do not have much time to spend in the kitchen.

Pressure Cooking Tips

Possibly the biggest hurdle in pressure cooking is overcoming the intimidation you feel when you pull it out of the box and see dozens of buttons. Meanwhile, memories of exploding pressure cookers suddenly surface and you're wondering whether your purchase was a wise one. Rest assured, modern electric pressure cookers are very safe, and the best way to overcome the intimidation from the many functions and settings is to jump in and start using it. (Says the girl who nervously waited three weeks to pull it out of the box. We all start somewhere, right?)

All electric pressure cookers and multicookers come with a user manual, but I want to give you a few tips to get you started and learn how to get the most out of the recipes in this cookbook.

Function and Size

You've probably noticed that electric pressure cookers aren't just pressure cookers anymore, but can also be used as a slow cooker, yogurt maker, and steamer. Generally, they have a sauté mode, which is incredibly useful for searing meat or cooking off liquid after the pressure cooker cycle without having to dirty an extra pan. Using fewer dishes is always a good thing.

Multicookers also have anywhere from six to ten special function buttons, depending on which model you have, like "Rice," "Soup," "Eggs," etc. Treat these buttons like you would the preprogrammed buttons on your microwave. Sometimes, they're good to use, but they don't always give you the results you want. Luckily, these settings are adjustable and you can tweak the cook time to meet your needs. For the recipes in this book, I always use the "Manual" or "Pressure Cook" button. It might be under a different name, but it isn't a preprogrammed setting.

All of these recipes were tested using 6-quart (5.7 L) Instant Pot brand pressure cookers. I find the 6-quart (5.7 L) cooker to be the best option for a midsize family. If you have a 5-quart (4.7 L), you'll probably be fine with most of the recipes, but if you have a 3-quart (2.8 L), you'll have to cut the recipes in half. For 8-quart (7.6 L) users, you may have to add some extra liquid if you feel the recipe doesn't have enough or even double the recipe to ensure that the pot will build pressure.

Natural vs. Manual Pressure Release

Another important aspect of pressure cooking is steam or pressure release. You'll see it mentioned in every recipe, either to naturally or manually release pressure. What does this mean?

Natural Release

Natural pressure release means that you don't need to touch anything and the cooker will gently release the pressure on its own. The nice thing about electric cookers is that once the pressure-cooking cycle is finished, another timer will begin to let you know how long it has been since the cycle has stopped and the cooker has been releasing pressure.

This method is very convenient, but keep in mind that your food will continue to cook for at least 10–15 minutes after the pressure cycle has ended as it gently releases pressure. This is fine if you're making a big pot roast (actually preferred, as it creates more tender, juicy meat), but not if you're steaming broccoli.

Manual Release

Manual pressure release is when you release the pressure yourself by switching the pressure release valve (located on the lid) from "Sealing" to "Venting." Do this carefully, as a strong blast of steam will erupt from the steam valve. You can place a folded kitchen towel over the valve to catch the steam if you like. It will help protect your kitchen cabinets from being steamed to death.

This method is nice if you're in a hurry or trying not to overcook something (like broccoli or eggs), but keep in mind that there's a lot of action going on inside the pot during a manual release. If you don't want your food jostled around a lot (e.g., a quiche), then you might want to use the natural release method first.

Most of the time, I use a combination of the two methods. I let the cooker come down naturally for a few minutes, and then I release the rest of the pressure with a manual release. (Times are noted in each recipe for pressure release.) Also, if you're making soup or something with a lot of liquid, it would be wise to use the natural release method first so you don't have liquid splattering up through the steam valve. It isn't pretty.

Using Thickeners

Typically, when you make a sauce or a soup, you add a thickener (like a type of starch) near the beginning of the process and build your recipe from there. When you use a pressure cooker, sauces and soups need to be thickened at the end. This is because the starch from thickeners can create foam inside the pot and possibly splatter out of the steam valve or stick to the bottom of the pot.

To thicken a soup or a sauce, it's easiest to make a slurry of water and your desired starch (I use tapioca and arrowroot powder the most) and add it at the end, after pressure has been released. You may need to turn the pot to the sauté setting to bring the liquid back up to a simmer, if necessary.

Searing with the Sauté Mode

Not needing an additional pan to sear meat has been such a convenience! To get the best results when searing cuts of meat or meatballs, make sure the pot has completely preheated before you put the meat in. Most cookers should give you a notification when the pot has preheated. And be sure to add enough oil or fat to the pot, too, especially if your pressure cooker pot is stainless steel.

Another tip (which also applies to searing on the stovetop) is to leave the meat alone when you put it in the pot. Seriously, don't touch it for at least 3–4 minutes unless you suspect it might be burning. You'll have a much easier time flipping steaks and turning meatballs this way.

Recommended Equipment

Besides the usual kitchen essentials, like tongs and a sturdy, thin spatula, there are a few other things that you might enjoy having if you use your pressure cooker often.

Pressure Cooker Accessories

I highly recommend purchasing extra silicone rings and vent seals for your pressure cooker lid and replacing them as needed. These silicone pieces absorb a lot of odor from the food you cook, and it's nearly impossible to completely remove the smell. Most of the time, it isn't an issue, especially if the food-like smell doesn't bother you, but if you have an old, pungent ring from making weekly Indian curry, you might not want to use the same ring to make custard because of possible flavor transfer. You could also keep two rings and reserve one for mild foods like desserts, potatoes, and eggs.

Also available are additional insert pots and plastic lids that fit over the pots if you prefer to use the insert pots to store leftovers.

Poaching Cups

Another handy, inexpensive accessory I found are silicone poaching cups. If you're a fan of poached eggs, but struggle to make them well, then these are a must-have. See my Poached Eggs (page 95) recipe, where I explain a little more how to use them.

Baking Equipment

If you plan to use your pressure cooker to bake, I highly recommend some scaled-down baking pans and ramekins to make desserts. Anything 7 inches (17.5 cm) wide or smaller will fit in a 6-quart (5.7 L) instant pot. My favorite pan is a 7-inch (17.5 cm) springform, which makes removing cakes much easier than a 7-inch (17.5 cm) baking pan, but either one will work in a pressure cooker.

A set of 6-ounce (175 ml) ramekins are also useful for making custards and puddings. You can also use 1-pint (475 ml) canning jars for this or other containers that are heat-safe and similar in size.

Paleo Pantry Staples

These are a few staples I like to keep on hand when making replacements for things like soy sauce, Worcestershire sauce, hard grated cheese, flours, and cooking oils. Once you use them a couple of times, it'll feel like second nature having them stocked in your pantry all the time.

Ghee

Ghee is simply butter with the milk solids removed. You can buy ghee at some grocery stores or online, or you can make it yourself. It's easy (see Homemade Ghee, page 234). Ghee adds a delicious buttery flavor to sauces or to seared meat, and because the milk solids have been removed, it will no longer burn when heated to higher temperatures.

Coconut Aminos

This one appears quite often in this book. Coconut aminos (not to be confused with soy-based liquid aminos) is a coconut-based umami-boosting ingredient and can be used as a soy sauce or Worcestershire sauce substitute. It's not as potent as soy sauce, so you'll need to use about 50 percent more if you are substituting for soy sauce. You can find coconut aminos online, at natural grocery stores, and even at some well-stocked traditional grocers.

Nutritional Yeast

This is simply dried, deactivated yeast and gives recipes a "cheesy" flavor. I use it often in dips or other recipes that would normally rely on cheese as a main flavor. This can also be found in natural grocery stores, online, and at some traditional grocery stores.

Grain-Free Flours

Tapioca flour (and cassava flour) is starch extracted from the cassava root and arrowroot is derived from several tropical plants. Both are neutral tasting and can be used interchangeably. They're great for thickening, emulsifying, and using in grain-free baking.

Blanched almond flour is finer than regular almond flour or meal and is made from almonds that have had their skins removed. It can be found in many grocery stores and online.

Palm Shortening

Palm shortening is my favorite substitute for regular vegetable shortening. It is made from palm oil, is flavorless, and acts like vegetable shortening in recipes, creating a fluffy, biscuit-like texture in recipes such as the Spiced Apple Cobbler (page 213). It's available in natural grocery stores, some well-stocked traditional stores, and online. My favorite place to purchase it is at TropicalTraditions.com because of their sustainable sourcing practices.

1

APPETIZERS AND DRINKS

Not only can you make party offerings quickly and easily in your pressure cooker, but you can also transport them well because the lid seals! No more sloshed hot chocolate or BBQ sauce in the backseat of your car. And reheating dips and drinks is a snap using the sauté setting.

Recipes

Chili Cheeze Dip

When I was a kid, I loved mom's chili cheese dip—a simple concoction of chili con carne and Mexican cheese sauce that would drain a bag of tortilla chips faster than anything else. I created a paleo-friendly version of my favorite party dip that was met with lip smacks and finger licks and sighs of disappointment when the bowl was scraped clean.

Prep time 15 minutes
Pressure time 5 minutes
Serves 8-10

1 tablespoon (15 ml) bacon drippings, ghee (page 234), or avocado oil

1 pound (455 g) ground beef

1 pound (455 g) ground pork

1 tablespoon (10 g) minced garlic

2 tablespoons (15 g) chili powder

2 teaspoons onion powder

1 teaspoon ground cumin

1 teaspoon hot paprika

1 teaspoon sea salt

1 bell pepper, any color, seeded and diced

One 6-ounce (170 g) can tomato paste

2 cups (475 ml) beef broth, homemade (page 242) or store-bought

1½ cups (355 ml) Spicy Nacho Sauce (page 240)

1 Turn the cooker to the high sauté setting and add your fat of choice. When the cooker has preheated, add the ground meats. Cook, breaking it into bits, until the meat is fully cooked and begins to form crispy edges.

2 Add the rest of the ingredients (except the Spicy Nacho Sauce) and stir well.

3 Cover the cooker and close the steam valve. Set it to high pressure for 5 minutes. Release the pressure manually. The texture of the dip should be similar to an extra-thick chili. If there seems to be an excess of moisture in the dip, cook it on the sauté setting for a few minutes to cook off some of that liquid.

4 Transfer the chili dip to a large serving bowl. Drizzle the Spicy Nacho Sauce into the chili dip. You can either leave it swirled together or mix it together completely.

5 Serve with vegetable sticks, mini bell peppers, and/or baked vegetable chips.

Middle Eastern Eggplant Hummus

Eggplant is such a funny vegetable, with its foamy texture and dolphin-like skin. It really shines when it's cooked and blended with tahini, fresh lemon juice, and my Middle Eastern Seasoning blend—a legume-free alternative to hummus.

Prep time 5 minutes
Pressure time 5 minutes
Makes about 2½ cups (600 g)

3 tablespoons (45 ml) avocado oil

3 large cloves of garlic, smashed

½ teaspoon ground cumin

1½ teaspoons Middle Eastern Seasoning (page 245)

1 large eggplant, trimmed and cut into 2-inch (5 cm) pieces (peeling optional)

¼ cup (60 ml) chicken broth, homemade (page 242) or store-bought, or water

⅓ cup (80 g) tahini

3 tablespoons (45 ml) freshly squeezed lemon juice

3 tablespoons (45 ml) extra-virgin olive oil

1 Put the avocado oil in the cooker and set it to high sauté. When the pot has preheated, add the garlic, cumin, and Middle Eastern Seasoning. Cook for a minute and then add the eggplant, stirring to coat it in the spiced oil. Add the chicken broth.

2 Cover the pot and close the steam valve. Set the cooker to high pressure for 5 minutes. Release the pressure manually when it finishes.

3 Transfer the eggplant and any pot juices to a blender or food processor. Add the tahini, lemon juice, and olive oil. Blend until smooth. Taste and add a pinch of salt or a squeeze of lemon, if needed.

4 Transfer the dip to a serving bowl and serve warm or at room temperature with crudités.

Creamy Salmon and Caper Dip

This creamy salmon dip can easily double as a salad! I love making a batch at the beginning of the week and pulling it out for a quick lunch alongside some bell pepper chunks or plantain chips or spooned into lettuce cups.

Prep time 15 minutes
Pressure time 4 minutes
Makes about 3 cups (710 g)

1 pound (454 g) fresh salmon fillets

½ teaspoon sea salt, divided

Generous pinch of black pepper

2 teaspoons minced garlic, divided

2 large lemons, divided

1 tablespoon (15 ml) melted ghee (page 234) or grass-fed butter

1 cup (225 g) Paleo-Friendly Mayonnaise (page 230), divided

2 heaping tablespoons (8 g) chopped fresh dill or ½ teaspoon dried dill

1 tablespoon (9 g) capers, chopped

1 tablespoon (4 g) nutritional yeast (optional)

4 scallions, thinly sliced

1 Prepare your cooker by putting 1 cup (235 ml) of water in the insert pot as well as the wire rack. Put the salmon fillets on the wire rack and sprinkle them with ¼ teaspoon of the salt, the pepper, and 1 teaspoon of the minced garlic.

2 Cut one of the lemons into slices and put 3–4 slices on the salmon. Drizzle the ghee over the salmon and then close the lid and the steam valve.

3 Set the cooker to high pressure for 4 minutes. Use a quick release to manually release all the pressure.

4 Transfer the salmon to a plate. Remove the skin from the back and break up the salmon with a fork, checking to see if there are any bones. Transfer the salmon to a medium bowl.

5 Add 4 tablespoons (60 ml) of lemon juice from the other lemon, ⅔ cup (157 g) of the Paleo-Friendly Mayonnaise, dill, capers, nutritional yeast, scallions, the remaining 1 teaspoon of minced garlic, and the remaining ¼ teaspoon of salt.

6 Stir very well for a couple of minutes until the salmon is shredded finely and everything is thoroughly combined. Add a little more mayo, if you'd like the dip to be creamier.

7 Serve with crudités or spoon into lettuce cups for serving.

Buffalo Chicken Meatballs

I've always been more interested in the game day snack offerings than the actual sports event—whatever it might be. I'll shamelessly admit that I go for the food. These meatballs are a great addition to a game day spread and will please everyone, regardless of the degree of sports devotion.

Prep time 25 minutes

Pressure time 5 minutes +
5 minutes natural release

Makes about 24 meatballs

For the meatballs:

2 pounds (900 g) ground chicken or turkey

2 tablespoons (28 ml) cayenne pepper sauce

1 teaspoon all-purpose salt-free seasoning blend

1 teaspoon minced garlic

¾ teaspoon sea salt

½ teaspoon onion powder

½ cup (60 g) minced celery

½ cup (55 g) grated carrot

2 tablespoons (28 ml) avocado oil, divided

For the sauce:

½ cup (120 ml) cayenne pepper sauce

4 tablespoons (60 ml) melted ghee (page 234) or grass-fed butter

1 teaspoon minced garlic

1 teaspoon tapioca flour

¼ cup (60 ml) water

3 scallions, thinly sliced, for garnish

1 To make the meatballs, place the ground chicken in a medium bowl. Add the cayenne pepper sauce, seasoning blend, garlic, salt, onion powder, celery, and carrot and gently mix everything with your hands until thoroughly combined. Form the meat into about twenty-four 1½-inch (3.8 cm) meatballs and set them on a large plate.

2 Turn the cooker to the high sauté mode. Add 1 tablespoon (15 ml) of the avocado oil. When the pot has preheated, place half of the meatballs in the pot. Let them cook, undisturbed, for 3–4 minutes. Flip and brown the other side. (They don't have to cook all the way through.) Transfer them to a plate, add the remaining 1 tablespoon (15 ml) of avocado oil, and sear the other half of the meatballs. When

they are finished, turn the cooker off and add the reserved meatballs back to the pot.

3 To make the sauce, pour the ½ cup (120 ml) of cayenne pepper sauce, ghee, and garlic over the meatballs.

4 Cover the pot, close the valve, and set it to high pressure for 5 minutes. Let the pressure release naturally for 5 minutes and then release the rest of the pressure manually.

5 Transfer the meatballs to a serving bowl and cover to keep warm. Whisk the tapioca flour into the water and whisk it into the sauce. Turn the cooker to high sauté and simmer for a few minutes until the sauce thickens.

6 Pour the sauce over the meatballs and sprinkle the scallions over the top.

Pesto Meatballs with Balsamic Glaze

Pesto is such an easy way to flavor meatballs! My Paleo Pesto is cheese-free and gives these meatballs a punch of basil and garlic. For a fun variation, you can try the Sun-Dried Tomato Pesto from the recipe on page 195.

Prep time 30 minutes
Pressure time 5 minutes
+ 5 minutes natural release
Makes about 20 meatballs

1½ cups (355 ml) balsamic vinegar
1 pound (455 g) ground beef
1 pound (455 g) ground pork
⅔ cup (160 g) Paleo Pesto (page 231)
1 teaspoon minced garlic

1 teaspoon sea salt
2–3 tablespoons (28–45 ml) avocado oil, divided
½ cup (120 ml) chicken broth, homemade (page 242) or store-bought

1 Place the balsamic vinegar in a small saucepan and cook over medium-high heat for about 30 minutes until it has reduced to about ⅔ cup (160 ml) and has thickened. Let it cool.

2 Meanwhile, combine the beef, pork, Paleo Pesto, garlic, and salt in a medium bowl. Use your hands to gently combine everything thoroughly. Roll the mixture into tight ½-inch (3.8 cm) meatballs.

3 Turn the cooker to high sauté. When it is preheated, add 1 tablespoon (15 ml) of the avocado oil and brown the meatballs on both sides in three batches, adding more oil as needed. Let them cook for 3 minutes on each side undisturbed and then flip them. They don't have to be cooked all the way through.

4 When they're all browned, turn the cooker off and return all of the meatballs to the pot. You can drain off any grease if you like or just leave it in the pot. Either way is fine. Add the chicken broth to the pot.

5 Close the lid and the steam valve. Set the cooker to high pressure for 5 minutes. Let the cooker release the pressure naturally for 5 minutes and then release the rest of the pressure manually.

6 Transfer the meatballs to a serving platter and drizzle with the balsamic glaze.

Note: If you want to brown the meatballs faster, you can do it in a large skillet on the stove in fewer batches.

Smoky Turkey Meatballs with BBQ Sauce

These meatballs come together quickly as a party appetizer, but can double as a weeknight meal. Just roast a pan of vegetables or make some Roasted Cauliflower Rice (page 200) to serve with it! My kids loved these, and I have a feeling they'll be on frequent rotation at your house as well.

Prep time 30 minutes

Pressure time 5 minutes + 5 minutes natural release

Makes about 20 meatballs

Note: Browning turkey meatballs in your pressure cooker is easier if you wait until the cooker has preheated on the sauté setting completely before adding the meat.

4 tablespoons (60 ml) avocado oil

⅓ cup (55 g) minced sweet onion

1 jalapeño pepper, seeded and minced

1 teaspoon minced garlic

2 pounds (900 g) ground turkey or chicken

1½ teaspoons sea salt

1 teaspoon ground cumin

1 tablespoon (7 g) smoked paprika

2 limes

2–3 cups (470–710 ml) Smoky Maple BBQ Sauce (page 239) or Mango-Chile BBQ Sauce (page 235), divided

1 Turn the cooker to the medium sauté setting and add 1 tablespoon (15 ml) of the avocado oil. Add the onion, jalapeño, and garlic to the cooker. Cook, stirring occasionally, until the vegetables are tender, 5-7 minutes.

2 While the vegetables are cooking, place the ground turkey in a large bowl. Add the salt, cumin, paprika, and about 2 tablespoons (28 ml) of juice from one of the limes. When the sautéed vegetables are finished, add those to the turkey as well. Turn the cooker off.

3 Use your hands to gently blend the turkey mixture—avoid squeezing the meat in your fists. Form the turkey mixture into about twenty 1½-inch (3.8 cm) meatballs.

4 Turn the cooker back on to the high sauté setting and add another tablespoon (15 ml) of avocado oil. Wait until the cooker has preheated and then, in three batches, sear the meatballs on two sides until golden brown, adding a little avocado oil between batches, if needed. If the meatballs are hard to turn or start sticking badly, leave them alone and let them cook a little longer. They do not need to be cooked through at this point.

5 Turn the cooker off. Return all of the meatballs to the pot and pour 1½ cups (355 ml) of the BBQ sauce over the meatballs.

6 Close the lid and the steam valve. Set the cooker to high pressure for 5 minutes. Allow the cooker to release pressure naturally for 5 minutes and then release the rest of the pressure manually.

7 Transfer the meatballs to a serving dish and cover to keep warm. Turn the cooker to the high sauté setting and cook the juices down for 4-5 minutes until slightly thickened. Add the rest of the BBQ sauce to your taste to the skillet and serve with the meatballs. Squeeze a little lime juice from the remaining lime over the meatballs before serving.

Quick and Easy BBQ Chicken Wings

Pressure cooking has made cooking wings so easy! They get incredibly tender so quickly. Just finish them off in the oven to crisp up the skin and have plenty of BBQ sauce (and napkins) to go with them.

Prep time 10 minutes

Pressure time 6 minutes + 10 minutes natural release + 10 minutes broiling time

Serves 8

1½ cups (355 ml) Smoky Maple BBQ Sauce (page 239) or your favorite BBQ sauce, divided

⅓ cup (80 ml) water

3 pounds (1.4 kg) chicken wings

1 teaspoon sea salt

¼ teaspoon black pepper

1 Pour ⅓ cup (80 ml) of the BBQ sauce and the water to the pot.

2 Put the wings in a large bowl and sprinkle with the salt and pepper; toss to coat. Place the wings in the pot with the sauce. Give it a stir to coat the wings in the BBQ sauce.

3 Close the lid and the steam valve and set the cooker to high pressure for 6 minutes. Let the cooker release the pressure on its own for 10 minutes before releasing the rest manually.

4 Preheat your oven broiler and line a large rimmed baking sheet with aluminum foil.

5 When the wings are finished, lay them in a single layer on the baking sheet. Broil on an upper oven rack for 10–15 minutes until the skin has crisped up. During the last few minutes, brush them with some of the remaining BBQ sauce, return them to the oven for a couple of minutes, and then brush them again.

6 Serve the wings with additional BBQ sauce and lots of napkins.

Smoky Hot Mixed Nuts

I love the subtle touch of sweetness from the pineapple juice in these nuts. It plays off of the hot sauce and steak seasoning so well to create a sticky, spicy coating. It's awfully hard to eat just a few!

Prep time 5 minutes

Pressure time 3 minutes + 10–15 minutes roasting time

Makes about 4 cups (600 g)

3 cups whole raw nuts ([300g] walnuts, [420 g] cashews, [300 g] pecans, [435 g] almonds)

⅔ cup (160 ml) unsweetened pineapple juice

⅓ cup (46 g) raw pepitas (pumpkin seeds)

⅓ cup (48 g) sunflower seeds

3 tablespoons (45 ml) melted coconut oil

2 tablespoons (28 ml) hot sauce

1 tablespoon (10 g) steak seasoning

1 Put all of the ingredients in the pot of your pressure cooker. Stir well.

2 Close the lid and the steam valve and set the cooker to high pressure for 3 minutes. Use a quick release to release the pressure.

3 Meanwhile, preheat your oven to 350°F (180°C, or gas mark 4) and line a rimmed baking sheet with parchment paper.

4 Transfer the nuts to the parchment paper and toast in the oven for 10–15 minutes, or until all of the moisture has cooked off and the nuts are toasted. Toss the nuts around with a spatula a couple of times during cooking.

5 Let them cool before serving.

Sweet and Spicy Teriyaki Wings

These sticky sweet wings are a great last-minute party appetizer—even if you don't have the teriyaki sauce made. The sauce comes together in about 5 minutes and you can have these ready to go in about 30 minutes!

Prep time 5 minutes

Pressure time 6 minutes + 10 minutes natural release + 10 minutes broiling time

Makes about 25 wings

1 cup (235 ml) Paleo Teriyaki Sauce (page 236), divided

½ cup (120 ml) water

3 pounds (1.4 kg) chicken wings and/or drummettes

2 teaspoons sea salt

¼ teaspoon black pepper

Pinch of crushed red pepper

1-2 tablespoons (15-30 g) sambal oelek or Asian chili garlic paste

1 tablespoon (20 g) honey

1 Put ¼ cup (60 ml) of the Paleo Teriyaki Sauce and the water in the pot. Add the wings, salt, black pepper, and red pepper. Mix to coat everything in the sauce.

2 Close the lid and the steam valve. Set the cooker to high pressure for 6 minutes. Let the pressure release naturally for 10 minutes before releasing the rest of the pressure manually.

3 While the wings are cooking, turn on your oven broiler and line a large rimmed baking sheet with aluminum foil. Combine the remaining ¾ cup (175 ml) Paleo Teriyaki Sauce with the sambal oelek (according to your heat preference) and honey.

4 When the wings are done, transfer them to the baking sheet and broil for 10-12 minutes, brushing them twice with the spicy teriyaki mixture toward the end of baking. The skin on the wings should be crispy with a coating of sticky sauce.

5 Serve the wings with the remaining sauce.

Sriracha Deviled Eggs

I always found it interesting that most deviled eggs aren't spicy. The word "deviled" conjures up images of redness and heat in my mind. While pickles and mustard are a fabulous pairing with eggs, I've always been a literal person, and these eggs are no exception. There is definitely redness and heat going on here.

Prep time 20 minutes
Pressure time 4 minutes
Makes 6 deviled eggs

8 eggs

2 tablespoons (28 g) Paleo-Friendly Mayonnaise (page 230)

1–2 tablespoons (15–28 ml) sriracha or (15-30 g) sambal oelek, to taste

Pinch of cayenne pepper

1 teaspoon lime juice

Pinch of sea salt

Toasted sesame seeds, for garnish

Scallions, thinly sliced, for garnish

1 Prepare the cooker by putting the wire rack on the bottom of the pot and adding 1 cup (235 ml) of water. Place the eggs on the wire rack. Close the lid and the steam valve and set the cooker to high pressure for 4 minutes. Release the pressure manually.

2 While the eggs are cooking, prepare an ice bath by filling a medium bowl with ice and cold water. When the eggs come out of the pot, immediately put them into the water bath. This helps them to not overcook and to cool quickly so you can peel them sooner (and more easily).

3 Peel the eggs and slice them in half lengthwise. Carefully remove the yolks from the eggs, keeping the white halves intact. Put the yolks in a small bowl and the whites on a serving dish.

4 When all of the yolks have been removed, add the Paleo-Friendly Mayonnaise, 1 tablespoon (15 ml) of the sriracha, cayenne pepper, lime juice, and salt to the bowl with the yolks. Mix well with a fork, mashing everything together until smooth. Taste and adjust the seasonings to your liking, adding more lime or salt or more sriracha for more heat.

5 Fill each cooked egg white cavity with a small spoonful of the spicy yolk mixture, using up all of the filling.

6 Sprinkle each egg with a pinch of sesame seeds and some scallions. Serve.

Apple-Cranberry Wassail

I've always preferred wassail over hot chocolate, given the option, and I love the extra tangy punch from the cranberry juice in this version. It's cozy, full of spices, and easy to keep warm and reheat when you serve it from the pressure cooker.

Prep time 5 minutes

Pressure time 5 minutes + 10 minutes natural release

Makes about 3 quarts (2.8 L)

2 quarts (1.9 L) unsweetened, unfiltered apple juice or cider

2 cups (475 ml) unsweetened pineapple juice

1 cup (235 ml) unsweetened cranberry juice

¼ cup (36 g) coconut sugar

5 whole cloves

3 whole cinnamon sticks

3 allspice berries

1 orange

1 Combine all the ingredients except the orange in your pressure cooker pot.

2 Use a vegetable peeler to get 4 large zest strips off your orange. Try not to get a lot of white pith. Add the strips to the cooker.

3 Close the lid, close the steam valve, and set it to cook on high pressure for 5 minutes. (It might take around 15 minutes for it to pressurize because there is so much liquid.) Allow it to release the pressure naturally for at least 10 minutes to avoid splattering. At this point, you can release the rest of the pressure manually or let it release on its own.

4 Serve warm.

Creamy Hot Chocolate for a Crowd

Making hot chocolate for a lot of people is sometimes a challenge when it needs to be portable, too. The nice thing about using a pressure cooker is that the lid seals, ensuring that the hot chocolate won't get splashed on the floor of your car during transit.

This version is extra creamy from the coconut milk, but doesn't have a strong coconut flavor. Adding the chai spice gives it an exotic twist!

Prep time 10 minutes

Pressure time 1 minute + 10 minutes natural release

Makes about 2½ quarts (2.4 L)

Three 13-ounce (370 g) cans full-fat coconut milk

4 cups (950 ml) water

¾ cup (60 g) unsweetened 100% cacao powder or cocoa powder

¾ cup preferred sweetener ([255 g] honey, [175 ml] maple syrup, [108 g]coconut sugar)

1 teaspoon vanilla extract

1 Add all of the ingredients (except the vanilla) to your pressure cooker pot. Whisk until no lumps remain.

2 Close the lid and the pressure valve. Set the cooker to high pressure for 1 minute. (It might take around 15 minutes for it to pressurize because there is so much liquid.) Let the pressure release naturally for 10 minutes before releasing the rest of the pressure manually.

3 Stir in the vanilla. You may want to let the pot sit with the lid off for several minutes to help cool it off. Serve warm.

Chai-spiced variation: Add 1 tablespoon (8 g) Chai Spice Blend (page 245) with the coconut milk.

Gingered Apple Cider

This is a unique twist on apple cider with a bite of ginger and creaminess from coconut milk and vanilla.

Prep time 10 minutes

Pressure time 2 minutes + 10 minutes natural release

Makes about 2 quarts (1.9 L)

2 quarts (1.9 L) unsweetened apple juice or cider

3-inch (7.5 cm) piece of ginger (about 1 inch [2.5 cm] wide), cut into slices (peeling not necessary)

1 lemon

1 cup (235 ml) coconut milk

2-3 tablespoons (40-60 g) honey

1 tablespoon (15 ml) vanilla extract

1 Put the cider and ginger slices into the pressure cooker pot. Slice the end off the lemon and cut two ½-inch (1.3 cm) slices from the lemon. Add the slices to the pot and reserve the rest of the lemon for another use.

2 Close the lid and the steam valve. Set the cooker for 2 minutes on high pressure. (It might take around 15 minutes for it to pressurize because there is so much liquid.) Let the cooker release pressure naturally for 10 minutes before releasing the rest of the pressure manually.

3 Remove the lemon and ginger slices from the pot and discard.

4 To the pot, add the coconut milk, 2 tablespoons (40 g) of honey, and the vanilla. Stir well and then taste and add the remaining 1 tablespoon (20 g) of honey if you think it needs it.

5 Serve warm.

SPLENDID SOUPS

2

I think pressure cookers especially excel in soup making, creating a "simmered all afternoon" flavor in a fraction of the amount of time. This chapter has soups for all tastes—light pureed soups, fresh brothy soups, and hearty comfort soups and chilis for the darkest days of winter.

Recipes

Turmeric Detox Broth

Turmeric is having a moment lately and has been praised for its anti-inflammatory and detoxifying qualities. I created a warming, healing broth you can sip if you are feeling under the weather or in need of a good internal cleansing. In addition to turmeric, this broth has nourishing bone broth along with several other ingredients to help boost your immune system during the dreaded cold and flu season.

Prep time 10 minutes

Pressure time 1 minute + 10 minutes natural release

Makes about 2 quarts (1.9 L)

2 quarts (1.9 L) high-quality chicken bone broth

4 teaspoons (20 ml) apple cider vinegar

1 tablespoon (8 g) freshly grated ginger

1 tablespoon (15 ml) freshly squeezed lemon juice

2 teaspoons ground turmeric or 1 tablespoon (8 g) grated turmeric root

½ teaspoon minced garlic

Generous pinches of sea salt, black pepper, and cayenne pepper

Raw or Manuka honey, for serving

1 Combine all of the ingredients (except the honey) in your pressure cooker pot.

2 Close the lid and the steam valve and set it for high pressure for 1 minute. Let the pressure release naturally for 10 minutes and then release the rest manually.

3 Serve in mugs with a drizzle of honey, if desired.

Notes:

• *You can make this and freeze it ahead of time to pull out for cold/flu season or whenever you're in need of some cleansing. You can also halve the recipe if you like.*

• *Be sure to add the black pepper, as it helps your body absorb the turmeric more easily.*

Pureed Zucchini Soup with Basil and Lemon

If you are overwhelmed with zucchini in the summertime, whip up a batch or two of this soup to put a dent in your zucchini harvest. It's a light, summertime meal, and it even freezes well!

Prep time 10 minutes

Pressure time 10 minutes + 10 minutes natural release

Serves 6

1 tablespoon (15 ml) ghee (page 234) or avocado oil

1 large shallot, minced

1 quart (946 ml) vegetable or chicken broth, homemade (page 242) or store-bought

1½–2 pounds (680–900 g) zucchini, trimmed and cut into 1-inch (2.5 cm) pieces

1 pound (455 g) red or Yukon gold potatoes, cut into 1-inch (2.5 cm) cubes

2 teaspoons minced garlic

1 teaspoon sea salt

4 sprigs of fresh thyme leaves or ¼ teaspoon dried thyme

Zest and juice of 1 large lemon (keep separate)

1 small bunch of fresh basil, leaves removed

1 Set the cooker to sauté over high heat. Add the ghee to the pot. When the cooker has preheated, add the shallot. Sauté for 2–3 minutes.

2 Add the broth, zucchini, potatoes, garlic, salt, thyme sprigs, and ½ teaspoon of lemon zest.

3 Close the lid and the steam valve. Set the cooker to high pressure for 10 minutes. Allow the pressure to release naturally for 10 minutes and then release the rest of the pressure manually.

4 Take out the thyme stems. Add the basil leaves and the lemon juice. Blend the soup using an immersion blender or in batches using a countertop blender.

5 Taste and add more lemon juice or salt, as needed.

6 Serve.

Notes: If you're watching your carbs or avoiding potatoes, you can substitue an equal amount of cauliflower florets for the potato.

Creamy Garlic Almond Soup with Scallions

This creamy soup is one of my favorite pureed soups. The almonds create a rich, yet light-tasting soup, but honestly, it's all a vehicle for the garlic. No, that's not a typo. There really are 12 cloves in this soup, but after it cooks, mellows, and blends together, it'll be your favorite soup, too.

Prep time 15 minutes

Pressure time 5 minutes + 10 minutes natural release

Serves 6

2 tablespoons (28 ml) ghee (page 234) or grass-fed butter

1 cup (160 g) chopped sweet onion

1 shallot, diced

3 celery stalks, diced

12 cloves of garlic, smashed

1 medium white potato, diced

1 cup (145 g) whole raw almonds

1 teaspoon sea salt

1 quart (946 ml) vegetable or chicken broth, homemade (page 242) or store-bought

Juice from 1 large lemon

1 bunch of scallions, thinly sliced, for serving

Black pepper, for serving

1 Turn the cooker to the high sauté setting and add the ghee to the pot. When it has preheated, add the onion, shallot, celery, and garlic. Cook for about 5 minutes, stirring often, until the vegetables are tender and the onions are translucent.

2 Add the potato, almonds, salt, and broth to the pot.

3 Close the lid and the steam valve. Set it to high pressure for 5 minutes. Let the cooker release pressure naturally for 10 minutes before releasing the rest manually.

4 Blend the soup in a couple of batches using a high-powered countertop blender. Return the soup to the pot and add the lemon juice. Taste and add more salt, if needed.

5 Serve with a sprinkle of scallions and a generous pinch or two of pepper.

Notes:

• *If you happen to have some Paleo Pesto (page 231) lying around, it is a fabulous garnish for this soup!*

• *I recommend using a high-powered blender here instead of an immersion blender because it does a better job of breaking down the nuts and making the soup extra smooth.*

Simple Butternut Squash Soup

I really enjoy the convenience of buying cubed butternut squash, but I've noticed it doesn't have a very long fridge life. Luckily, you can throw this soup together easily when you've got a container on the verge of being a science project or if you simply need a light, quick dinner on a weeknight.

Prep time 5 minutes

Pressure time 10 minutes + 10 minutes natural release

Serves 6

2 tablespoons (28 ml) ghee (page 234)

1 cup (160 g) chopped sweet onion

1 teaspoon minced garlic

2 pounds (900 g) cubed butternut squash

1 quart (946 ml) chicken broth, home-made (page 242) or store-bought

½ teaspoon sea salt

3–4 sprigs of fresh thyme or ¼ teaspoon dried thyme

¼ teaspoon black pepper

One 11-ounce (310 g) can full-fat coconut milk

Juice from ½ lemon (about 2 tablespoons [28 ml])

1 Set the cooker to high sauté and add the ghee. When the cooker has preheated, add the onion and garlic to the pot. Sauté for 2–3 minutes until the onion is soft and translucent.

2 Add the squash, chicken broth, salt, thyme, and pepper to the pot.

3 Close the lid and the steam valve. Set the cooker to high pressure for 10 minutes. Let the cooker release pressure naturally for 10 minutes and then manually release the rest.

4 Remove the lid. Remove and discard the thyme stems. Blend the soup using an immersion blender or in batches using a countertop blender. The soup should be super smooth.

5 Stir in the coconut milk and lemon juice. Taste and add more salt or lemon juice if you feel it needs it.

6 Serve.

Note: This can easily be made vegan by using avocado oil and vegetable broth in place of the ghee and chicken broth.

Azteca Squash Soup with Chorizo

This recipe was adapted from one I found in a magazine years ago. I love our addition of chorizo, which makes the soup heartier and adds a delightful punch of spice. It's getting increasingly easier to find clean chorizo, but if you have trouble tracking some down, feel free to substitute any other spicy, precooked sausage.

Prep time 20 minutes

Pressure time 10 minutes + 10 minutes natural release

Serves 6

2 tablespoons (28 ml) avocado oil

1 medium sweet onion, diced

3 celery stalks, diced

1 red bell pepper, seeded and diced

2 teaspoons minced garlic

1 teaspoon ground cumin

1 teaspoon dried thyme

2½–3 pounds (1.1–1.4 kg) cubed acorn, kabocha, or butternut squash

1 quart (946 ml) chicken broth, home-made (page 242) or store-bought

1½ teaspoons sea salt

10–12 ounces (280–340 g) chorizo, diced or crumbled

1 lime

Chopped fresh cilantro, for serving

1 Set the cooker to high sauté and add the avocado oil. When the cooker has preheated, add the onion, celery, bell pepper, garlic, cumin, and thyme. Cook for 2–3 minutes until the onion is soft and translucent.

2 Add the squash cubes, chicken broth, and salt.

3 Close the lid and the steam valve. Set the cooker to high pressure for 10 minutes. Let the pressure release naturally for 10 minutes and then release the rest manually.

4 Meanwhile, cook the chorizo in a skillet until golden brown and hot.

5 Blend the soup with an immersion blender or in batches in a countertop blender.

6 Add the juice from half of the lime. Taste and add more lime juice or salt if necessary.

7 Serve with a sprinkle of fresh cilantro and a couple spoonfuls of sautéed chorizo.

Butternut Squash and Carrot Soup with Ginger

This recipe was originally a stovetop version that a former blogger, Lisa Thiele, guest posted on my website several years ago. It has become a favorite of my readers, and I wanted to share it here as well. I tweaked it, adapting it for the pressure cooker, and now it's easier than ever to get this smooth, gingery soup on the table.

Prep time 15 minutes

Pressure time 10 minutes + 10 minutes natural release

Serves 6

1 tablespoon (15 ml) avocado oil

1 cup (160 g) diced yellow onion

1½ pounds (680 g) cubed butternut squash

4 medium carrots, peeled and cut into 1-inch (2.5 cm) chunks

1 tablespoon (6 g) chopped ginger

1 teaspoon minced garlic

½ teaspoon sea salt

¼ teaspoon ground nutmeg

¼ teaspoon black pepper

1 quart (946 ml) vegetable broth

1 Turn the cooker to the high sauté setting. Add the avocado oil. When the cooker is preheated, add the onion and sauté until tender and translucent, about 5 minutes.

2 Add the rest of the ingredients to the pot.

3 Close the lid and the steam valve. Set the cooker for 10 minutes on high pressure. Allow the cooker to release the pressure naturally for 10 minutes and then you can release the rest manually, if you wish.

4 Remove the lid and blend the soup with an immersion blender or in batches using a countertop blender. The soup should be very smooth.

5 Serve.

Easy Tomato Soup

This soup is especially good in the summer at the height of tomato season. Sweet, ripe tomatoes make this soup extra special and will help use up some of those tomatoes exploding out of your garden. It also freezes well!

Prep time 10 minutes

Pressure time 5 minutes + 10 minutes natural release

Serves 8-10

3 tablespoons (45 ml) ghee (page 234), divided

1 large sweet onion, diced

6 cloves of garlic, smashed

3 pounds (1.4 kg) vine tomatoes, quartered

1 pound (455 g) cherry or grape tomatoes

4-5 sprigs of fresh thyme or 1 teaspoon dried thyme

1 cup (235 ml) chicken broth, homemade (page 242) or store-bought

2 tablespoons (32 g) tomato paste

2 teaspoons sea salt

¼ teaspoon black pepper

1 cup (235 ml) coconut milk

Nutritional yeast, for serving

1 Put 1 tablespoon (15 ml) of the ghee in the pot and set the cooker to the high sauté setting. When it has preheated, add the onion. Cook for 4-5 minutes until the onion has softened and begun to turn golden brown. Add the garlic and cook for another minute or so.

2 Turn the cooker off. Add all of the tomatoes, thyme, chicken broth, tomato paste, salt, and pepper.

3 Close the lid and the steam valve. Set the cooker to high pressure for 5 minutes. Let the cooker release pressure naturally for 10 minutes and then release the rest of the pressure manually.

4 Remove the lid and fish out the thyme stems. Blend the soup using an immersion blender or in batches with a countertop blender.

5 Add the coconut milk and the remaining 2 tablespoons (28 ml) of ghee. Taste and add more salt, if necessary.

6 Serve with a sprinkle of nutritional yeast and a few cranks of freshly ground black pepper.

Note: The Bacon-Onion Jam (page 120) or Paleo Pesto (page 231) is fabulous in this soup.

Easy Egg Drop Soup

If I had known just how easy egg drop soup was, I would have started making it years ago! The chicken broth you use will determine how tasty this soup turns out, so be sure to use a high-quality brand or even better, make some Homemade Chicken Broth (page 242) yourself!

Prep time 5 minutes

Pressure time 5 minutes + 10 minutes natural release

Serves 6

2 quarts (1.9 L) chicken broth, homemade (page 242) or store-bought

¼ cup (60 ml) coconut aminos

2 tablespoons (28 ml) sesame oil

2-inch (5 cm) knob of ginger, finely grated

½ teaspoon minced garlic

1½ teaspoons sea salt

2 eggs

5 scallions, thinly sliced, for serving

1 Put the chicken broth, coconut aminos, sesame oil, ginger, garlic, and salt in the pot.

2 Close the lid and the steam valve. Set the cooker to high pressure for 5 minutes. Let the pressure naturally release for 10 minutes and then release the rest manually.

3 Whisk the eggs in a small bowl. Take the lid off the cooker and while stirring the broth in one circular direction, slowly drizzle in the whisked eggs.

4 Serve with a generous sprinkle of scallions.

Thai Chicken Zoodle Soup

This is a Thai-inspired take on traditional chicken noodle soup with common Thai ingredients like ginger, fish sauce, and lemongrass. You'll love the zucchini noodles and fresh herbs in this. Don't skimp on the fresh herbs—they take this soup to a whole other level!

Prep time 15 minutes

Pressure time 10 minutes + 10 minutes natural release

Serves 6

Note: For more heat, you can add a minced Thai chile or a jalapeño pepper with the ingredients in step 2.

1 tablespoon (14 g) coconut oil

12 ounces (340 g) chicken breasts or thighs, cut into 1-inch (2.5 cm) pieces

Sea salt

2 quarts (1.9 L) chicken broth, homemade (page 242) or store-bought, divided

2 large carrots, peeled and sliced into ¼-inch (6 mm) pieces

1 shallot, diced

1 teaspoon minced garlic

2 tablespoons (12 g) minced ginger

5 ounces (140 g) shiitake mushrooms, sliced

3 tablespoons (45 ml) fish sauce

1 stalk of lemongrass

1 zucchini, thinly spiralized

2-3 tablespoons (28-45 ml) lime juice (2 juicy limes)

½ cup (8 g) chopped fresh cilantro

¼ cup (10 g) chopped fresh basil

¼ cup (24 g) chopped fresh mint

Asian chili paste or sambal oelek, for serving

1 Set the cooker to the high sauté mode. Add the coconut oil. When it has preheated, sprinkle the chicken with a couple of generous pinches of salt and sear the chicken on both sides, 3-4 minutes each, until a golden crust forms.

2 Add ½ cup (120 ml) of the chicken broth to the pot to deglaze the bottom—scrape loose any bits that have gotten stuck as it bubbles. Add the remaining chicken broth along with the carrots, shallot, garlic, ginger, mushrooms, and fish sauce.

3 Lay the lemongrass stalk on a countertop. Smash it using your fist over the flat side of your knife or use a meat tenderizer—just enough to break it up slightly. (This allows the lemongrass to more easily release its flavor.) Cut the stalk into 3 pieces and add them to the pot.

4 Close the lid and the steam valve and set the cooker to high pressure for 10 minutes. Allow the cooker to release the pressure naturally for 10 minutes and then release the rest of the pressure manually, if you wish.

5 Remove the lid and immediately add the spiralized zucchini, lime juice, and fresh herbs. Stir, cover with the lid, and let it sit for 5 minutes to allow the zucchini noodles to cook.

6 Remove the lemongrass pieces. Taste and add more lime juice or salt, if needed.

7 Serve with Asian chili paste.

Cashew Chicken Curry Soup with Bok Choy and Carrot Ribbons

Bok choy is a common vegetable in Asian cooking, and if you haven't used it, I highly recommend it! It's found in most grocery stores and is similar to cabbage and dark greens in texture. It also stands up well to the punch of flavors in this curry-like soup.

Prep time 15 minutes

Pressure time 5 minutes + 5 minutes natural release

Serves 6

1 tablespoon (14 g) coconut oil

1 pound (455 g) chicken breasts or thighs, cut into ½-inch (1.3 cm) pieces

1 cup (160 g) diced yellow onion

2 medium heads of bok choy, trimmed and sliced

1 tablespoon (8 g) grated ginger

2 teaspoons ground turmeric

1 teaspoon sea salt

½ teaspoon ground coriander

⅔ cup (93 g) raw, unsalted cashew pieces

1 quart (946 ml) chicken broth, homemade (page 242) or store-bought

1 very large carrot, for carrot ribbons

One 13-ounce (370 g) can full-fat coconut milk

3 tablespoons (23 g) tapioca flour

1 tablespoon (15 ml) freshly squeezed lime juice

½ cup (8 g) chopped fresh cilantro

1 Set the cooker to high sauté and add the coconut oil to the pot. When the cooker has preheated, add the chicken to the pot and let it cook, undisturbed, for 3-4 minutes.

2 Add the onion and continue to sauté, stirring often, until the onion is soft and translucent.

3 Add the bok choy, ginger, turmeric, salt, coriander, cashews, and chicken broth to the pot.

4 Close the lid and the steam valve. Set the cooker to high pressure for 5 minutes. Let the cooker release the pressure naturally for 5 minutes and then release the rest of the pressure manually.

5 Make some carrot ribbons by laying the carrot on a flat surface and using a vegetable peeler to make wide, thin ribbons. Set the ribbons aside.

6 Remove the lid and turn the cooker to the sauté setting. Whisk together the coconut milk and tapioca flour. Stir it into the soup. Let it simmer for a minute or two until it has thickened.

7 Turn the cooker off and add the lime juice, cilantro, and carrot ribbons. Place the lid back on the pot and let it sit for 5 minutes or so to allow the carrot ribbons to soften.

8 Taste and add more salt or lime juice if needed.

9 Serve.

Greek Lemon Chicken Soup with Kale

My favorite part of making this soup is stirring in the whisked eggs and lemon juice at the end and seeing the broth take on a creamy, pale yellow color. Be sure to use fresh lemons here, as the flavor will be superior to store-bought lemon juice.

Prep time 20 minutes

Pressure time 5 minutes + 10 minutes natural release

Serves 6

1 tablespoon (15 ml) avocado oil

1½ teaspoons sea salt, divided

¾ teaspoon dried oregano

1½ pounds (680 g) boneless, skinless chicken breasts or thighs, cut into 1-inch (2.5 cm) pieces

½ cup (80 g) diced sweet onion

½ cup (50 g) chopped celery (about 2 stalks)

2–3 lemons (zest and ⅓ cup [80 ml] juice)

2 teaspoons minced garlic

2 quarts (1.9 L) chicken broth, homemade (page 242) or store-bought

1 bunch of kale, stems removed and leaves chopped (4 cups [268 g] tightly packed)

2 eggs

½ cup (30 g) chopped fresh Italian flat-leaf parsley

1 Turn the cooker to high sauté. Add the avocado oil.

2 Sprinkle 1 teaspoon of the salt and the oregano on the chicken. When the cooker has preheated, add the chicken to the pot and sear for 4–5 minutes, flipping it around occasionally.

3 Add the onion and celery to the pot as well as ½ teaspoon of finely grated lemon zest, the garlic, the remaining ½ teaspoon of salt, and the chicken broth. Add the kale and stir well.

4 Close the lid and the steam valve and set the cooker to high pressure for 5 minutes. Let the cooker release pressure naturally for 10 minutes and then manually release the rest of the pressure.

5 Meanwhile, whisk the lemon juice and eggs in a small bowl.

6 When the soup is finished, slowly ladle a cup (235 ml) of the soup broth into the egg-lemon mixture while whisking constantly. Now, pour that mixture back into the pot with the rest of the soup and mix well. If you have trouble getting all of the egg to cook, turn the cooker to the high sauté setting and simmer for just a minute. The soup should take on a creamy look and have a pronounced lemon flavor. Taste and add more salt or lemon juice if necessary.

7 Stir in the parsley and serve.

Creamy Southwest Chicken Soup

This soup was somewhat unintentional. I was in the mood for chicken soup, but found myself reaching for limes and green chiles and ended up with a Southwest version of chicken soup with some creaminess from a can of coconut milk. It quickly became a family favorite and a favorite of my readers when I shared it on my website.

Prep time 15 minutes

Pressure time 20 minutes + 5 minutes natural release

Serves 8

1½ teaspoons sea salt, divided

1 teaspoon ground cumin

1 teaspoon granulated garlic

1 teaspoon chili powder

2 pounds (900 g) boneless, skinless chicken breasts or thighs

4 tablespoons (60 ml) avocado oil

1 large onion, diced

4 medium carrots, diced

4 celery stalks, diced

2 bell peppers (any color), seeded and diced

Two 4-ounce (115 g) cans diced green chiles

6 cups (1.4 L) chicken broth, homemade (page 242) or store-bought

One 13.5-ounce (385 g) can full-fat coconut milk

2 tablespoons (28 ml) freshly squeezed lime juice, plus additional limes for serving

⅔ cup (11 g) chopped fresh cilantro, plus more for serving

Sliced avocado, for serving

Hot sauce, for serving

1 Combine the salt, cumin, garlic, and chili powder in a small bowl. Sprinkle both sides of the chicken with 2 teaspoons of the seasoning mixture.

2 Turn the cooker to the high sauté setting and add the avocado oil. When the pot is preheated, add the chicken. Sear it in the oil on both sides until a golden crust forms. It doesn't have to be cooked all the way through. Transfer to a plate and set side.

3 Add the onion, carrots, celery, and bell peppers to the pot. Cook, stirring to scrape up any bits of the chicken left behind. Put the chicken back in the pot along with the green chiles, chicken broth, and the rest of the seasoning mixture.

4 Put the lid on the cooker and close the steam valve. Set the cooker to high pressure for 20 minutes. Let the pressure release naturally for 5 minutes and then release the rest of the pressure manually.

5 Remove the lid. Remove the chicken from the pot, shred it, and return it to the pot.

6 Stir in the coconut milk, lime juice, and cilantro. Put the lid back on (don't seal it) for 5 minutes.

7 Serve with sliced avocado, hot sauce, lime wedges, and additional cilantro.

French Onion Beef Soup

It might take some extra time to caramelize the onions for this soup, but the result is well worth the time. Caramelized onions are one of nature's greatest magic tricks. Who knew that something as pungent as a raw onion could become as sweet as candy with a little time and heat?

Prep time 45 minutes

Pressure time 20 minutes + 15 minutes natural release

Serves 6

―――――――――

Note: If you like, you can cook the onions in a skillet on the stove while the meat is browning in the pressure cooker. You'll have an extra pan to clean, but everything will get prepped faster. Be sure to add a little broth to the skillet when you finish cooking the onions to scrape up any browned bits and transfer all of the onions and liquid from the pan to the pressure cooker in step 4.

2 teaspoons sea salt, divided

½ teaspoon onion powder

¼ teaspoon black pepper

1½ pounds (680 g) beef stew meat, cut into ½-inch (1.3 cm) pieces

4 tablespoons (60 ml) ghee (page 234), divided

4 large sweet onions, thinly sliced, divided

1½ quarts (1.4 L) beef broth, homemade (page 242) or store-bought, divided

4 sprigs of fresh thyme

2 teaspoons chopped fresh rosemary

¼ cup (60 ml) coconut aminos

1 tablespoon (15 ml) red wine vinegar (optional)

1 Combine 1 teaspoon of the salt, onion powder, and pepper in a small bowl. Sprinkle the mixture on the meat and toss to coat evenly.

2 Set the cooker to the high sauté mode. Add 1 tablespoon (15 ml) of the ghee to the pot. When the cooker has preheated, add half of the meat to the pot. Let it cook undisturbed for 2–3 minutes. Flip the meat around and cook a little longer until the meat is covered with golden brown spots. Transfer the meat to a bowl. Repeat with another tablespoon (15 ml) of ghee and the rest of the meat.

3 After the rest of the meat is removed from the pot, add another tablespoon (15 ml) of ghee and half of the onions. Cook, tossing the onions around with tongs, until they're very soft and golden brown, 10–12 minutes. Transfer the onions to the bowl with the beef and repeat with the remaining tablespoon (15 ml) of ghee and the rest of the onions.

4 Pour ½ cup (120 ml) of the beef broth into the pot and scrape the pot to release any bits that are stuck to the bottom. Add the remaining broth to the pot as well as the caramelized onions and beef. Add the fresh herbs, coconut aminos, and remaining teaspoon of salt.

5 Cover the pot and close the steam valve. Set the cooker to high pressure for 20 minutes. Let the cooker release pressure naturally for 15 minutes and if there is any pressure left, release it manually.

6 Taste the soup and adjust the salt, if needed. If the soup tastes a little flat, add the red wine vinegar.

7 Serve.

Cabbage Roll Soup

This simple, unassuming soup ended up being one of my favorites in this chapter. I especially love the sweet and sour effect in the broth from the honey and vinegar. I'd much rather whip up a batch of this easy soup than assemble cabbage rolls.

Prep time 20 minutes
Pressure time 5 minutes + 5 minutes natural release
Serves 8-10

1 tablespoon (15 ml) avocado oil

1 pound (455 g) ground beef

1 large sweet onion, diced

1 tablespoon (20 g) honey or (15 g) Date Paste (page 232)

One 28-ounce (785 g) can crushed tomatoes

1 teaspoon minced garlic

¼ cup (60 ml) white wine vinegar

2 tablespoons (32 g) tomato paste

1 small head of green cabbage, chopped into bite-size pieces

4 cups (946 ml) beef broth, homemade (page 242) or store-bought, divided

1 teaspoon sea salt

⅓ cup (20 g) chopped fresh parsley

1 Set the cooker to the high sauté mode and add the avocado oil. When it has preheated, add the ground beef. Cook, stirring often and breaking the meat into small bits, until it has crispy brown edges and the meat is beginning to stick to the bottom of the pot.

2 Add the onion and cook for another 2-3 minutes.

3 Stir in the honey, tomatoes, garlic, vinegar, tomato paste, cabbage, 3 cups (700 ml) of the beef broth, and salt.

4 Close the lid and the steam valve. Set the cooker to high pressure for 5 minutes. Let the cooker release the pressure naturally for 5 minutes and then release the rest of the pressure manually.

5 Stir in the parsley and if you'd like the soup to be thinner, add the remaining 1 cup (235 ml) of beef broth. Taste and adjust the salt and vinegar, if needed.

6 Serve.

40-Minute Steak Pho

This soup was a favorite of the recipe testers who helped me while I was writing this book and for good reason! I even got a "fantastic" out of my husband, who is very hard to impress. The blend of spices and homemade beef broth is so much better than any pho we've had in a restaurant. You can also make the broth alone and freeze it for even faster pho later in the month.

Prep time 20 minutes

Pressure time 5 minutes + 10 minutes natural release

Serves 6

2 quarts (1.9 L) beef broth, homemade (page 242) or store-bought

3 star anise pods

1-inch (2.5 cm) knob of ginger, sliced

1 cinnamon stick

1 teaspoon minced garlic

3 tablespoons (45 ml) coconut aminos

1 tablespoon (15 ml) fish sauce

1 teaspoon sea salt

8 ounces (225 g) uncooked frozen sirloin strip steak, very thinly sliced (¼ inch [6 mm] at most)

2–3 medium zucchini, spiralized

½ cup (8 g) chopped fresh cilantro

½ cup (20 g) fresh basil, thinly sliced

4 ounces (115 g) mung bean sprouts

2 limes, cut into wedges

Asian chili garlic paste, for serving

Jalapeño pepper, sliced, for serving

1 Put the beef broth, star anise, ginger, cinnamon, garlic, coconut aminos, fish sauce, and sea salt into the pot.

2 Close the lid and the steam valve and set the cooker to high pressure for 5 minutes. Let the cooker release pressure naturally for 10 minutes and then release the rest of the pressure manually.

3 While the broth is cooking, you'll have time to prep the steak, zucchini, and herbs.

4 When the broth is finished, fish out the spices and garlic with a spider skimmer or a slotted spoon. Discard them.

5 Add the beef and zucchini noodles to the broth while it is still piping hot. Put the lid on the pot (don't pressurize) and let it sit for 5 minutes or so to cook.

6 Ladle the soup into bowls and garnish with the fresh herbs, bean sprouts, a squeeze from a wedge of lime over the top, and a little Asian chili garlic paste and Jalapeño peppers if you like some heat.

7 Serve.

Note: Add an extra teaspoon of sea salt if using unsalted broth.

Tomatillo Beef and Zucchini Taco Soup

My mom made taco soup a lot when we were growing up, and it was always something I looked forward to. Her secret? Using ranch seasoning mix along with the taco seasoning. The ranch seasoning gives the soup an extra boost of flavor and more complexity. If you haven't tried my Dry Ranch Seasoning (page 236), I highly recommend it!

Prep time 20 minutes

Pressure time 5 minutes + 10 minutes natural release

Serves 6

1 pound (455 g) ground beef

4 tablespoons (30 g) taco seasoning

2 tablespoons (16 g) Dry Ranch Seasoning (page 237)

1 medium onion

1 tablespoon (10 g) minced garlic

One 15-ounce (425 g) can diced tomatoes

2 medium zucchini, halved lengthwise and chopped into ½-inch (1.3 cm) pieces

1 pound (455 g) fresh tomatillos, husks removed, chopped

1 bell pepper (any color), seeded and diced

1 large jalapeño, seeded (optional) and diced

2 cups (475 ml) beef broth, homemade (page 242) or store-bought

1 tablespoon (16 g) tomato paste

2 tablespoons (28 ml) lime juice (about ½ large juicy lime)

½ cup (8 g) chopped fresh cilantro

1 Turn the cooker to the high sauté setting and add the ground beef to the pot. Cook, breaking up the meat into small pieces, until the meat has crispy browned bits throughout.

2 Add the taco seasoning, Dry Ranch Seasoning, onion, and garlic and mix well. Cook for 2–3 minutes until the onion softens a little.

3 Add the diced tomatoes and stir everything together, scraping up the browned bits on the bottom of the pot.

4 Add the zucchini, tomatillos, bell pepper, jalapeño, beef broth, and tomato paste. Stir well.

5 Close the lid and the steam valve. Set the cooker to high pressure for 5 minutes. Let the cooker release pressure on its own for 10 minutes before releasing the rest manually.

6 Stir in the lime juice and the cilantro. Taste and add a little salt if necessary.

7 Serve.

Zuppa Toscana

This Olive Garden knockoff has a million variations on the Internet. I think there's room for a paleo-friendly, pressure cooker version, don't you? This is my favorite version. If you happen to be following a keto diet or are watching your carbs, feel free to substitute cauliflower florets for the russet potato.

Prep time 20 minutes

Pressure time 10 minutes + 5 minutes natural release

Serves 6

1 tablespoon (15 ml) avocado oil

1 pound (455 g) uncooked bulk Italian sausage

1 medium onion, chopped

2 teaspoons minced garlic

⅛ teaspoon crushed red pepper flakes

2 medium russet potatoes, peeled and cut into ½-inch (1.3 cm) cubes

1 bunch of fresh kale, stems removed and leaves cut into bite-size pieces

1½ quarts (1.4 L) chicken broth, home-made (page 242) or store-bought

2 tablespoons (28 ml) red wine vinegar

1 cup (235 ml) coconut milk

Salt and pepper, to taste

Chopped fresh parsley, for garnish

Crispy bacon, for garnish

1 Turn your pressure cooker to the high sauté setting. When it has pre-heated, add the avocado oil to the pot along with the sausage. Cook, breaking up the meat into little bits, for 10–15 minutes or until browned.

2 Add the onion, garlic, and red pepper flakes to the pot. Stir and cook for a minute or so. Add the potatoes, kale, chicken broth, and vinegar. Give it a stir.

3 Close the lid and the steam valve. Set it to high pressure for 10 minutes. You could cook up some bacon at this point if you plan on using it as a garnish. Let the cooker naturally release for 5 minutes and then release the remainder of the pressure manually.

4 Remove the lid. Add the coconut milk and about 1 teaspoon of salt and a grind of pepper. Give it a good stir and taste it, adding more salt or red wine vinegar if you feel it needs it.

5 Ladle into bowls and serve with the parsley and bacon.

Italian Sausage and Sauerkraut Soup

For a soup with such a short ingredients list, it sure has a lot of flavor. Sausage and sauerkraut is such a classic combination, and I love the extra flavor from the Italian sausage. You can certainly use bulk breakfast sausage if you like—we've tried it and they both work well.

Prep time 20 minutes

Pressure time 5 minutes + 5 minutes natural release

Serves 6

2 tablespoons (28 ml) ghee (page 234) or avocado oil

1 pound (455 g) bulk Italian sausage, sweet or spicy or a combination of the two

1 large onion, diced

2 cups (284 g) sauerkraut, rinsed

6 cups (1.4 L) chicken broth, homemade (page 242) or store-bought

2 tablespoons (30 g) Dijon mustard

1 Set the cooker to high sauté. Add the ghee. When it has melted and the cooker is heated, add the sausage. Cook, breaking the sausage up into small bits, until crispy edges have formed on the meat. Remove the sausage from the pot and set aside.

2 Add the onion, sauerkraut, chicken broth, and mustard to the pot and stir well.

3 Close the lid and the steam valve and set the cooker to high pressure for 5 minutes. Let the pressure release naturally for 5 minutes and then release the rest of the pressure manually, if you wish.

4 Add the sausage back to the soup and serve.

Cajun Sausage and Vegetable Stew

If you're like me and love skillet dinners with spicy andouille sausage and piles of dark leafy greens, you'll love this stew packed with loads of greens and other vegetables. I include a few side dish suggestions at the bottom, but honestly, I love eating it on its own.

Prep time 15 minutes
Pressure time 3 minutes
Serves 6

2 tablespoons (28 ml) ghee (page 234) or avocado oil

1 pound (455 g) andouille sausage, sliced into ½-inch (1.3 cm) pieces

1 cup (160 g) chopped sweet onion

2 celery stalks, diced

2 green bell peppers, seeded and diced

1 tablespoon (12 g) Cajun seasoning

½ cup (120 ml) broth (any kind), homemade (page 242) or store-bought

2 tablespoons (32 g) tomato paste

¼ cup (60 ml) apple cider vinegar

8 cups chopped dark leafy greens ([288 g] Swiss chard, [536 g] kale, [288 g] collards), about 2 large bunches

2 cups (224 g) frozen sliced okra or halved green beans

2 cups (300 g) halved cherry or grape tomatoes

1 Set the cooker to high sauté and add the ghee. When the pot has heated, add the pieces of sausage and cook for 2–3 minutes until they are warmed and have spots of golden brown on them.

2 Add the onion, celery, bell pepper, and Cajun seasoning. Cook, stirring often, until the onion has softened, 3–4 minutes. Pour in the broth and scrape the bottom of the pan to release any bits of sausage that may have stuck.

3 Stir in the tomato paste, vinegar, greens, okra, and tomatoes.

4 Close the lid and the steam valve. Set the cooker to high pressure for 3 minutes. Manually release all of the pressure when it has finished.

5 Serve with desired side dish.

Recommended side dishes: Cauliflower Puree with Rosemary and Garlic (page 201), Roasted Cauliflower Rice (page 200), or squash noodles

Notes:

• *If using fresh, uncooked andouille, put it in the freezer for an hour or so to make it easier to slice.*

• *Check your Cajun seasoning—if one of the first ingredients is salt, you might want to reduce the Cajun seasoning amount to 2 teaspoons.*

Charred Red Pepper Soup with Garlic Shrimp

Charring the red bell peppers for this soup takes a little time and effort, but it's well worth it. You could also char the peppers ahead of time and chill them until you're ready to make the soup. Also, if you're making the soup ahead of time, wait until just before you serve it to prepare the shrimp because they tend to get rubbery when they are reheated.

Prep time 30 minutes

Pressure time 5 minutes + 10 minutes natural release

Serves 6

For the shrimp:

1½ pounds (680 g) medium uncooked shrimp, peeled, tails removed, and thawed

Sea salt

1 large lime, divided

¼ cup (60 ml) melted ghee (page 234), grass-fed butter, or coconut oil

1 teaspoon minced garlic

Pinch of crushed red pepper flakes

For the soup:

6 red bell peppers

1 large jalapeño pepper

1 tablespoon (15 ml) ghee (page 234) or coconut oil

1 medium onion, chopped

2 large carrots, chopped

2 celery stalks, chopped

1 tablespoon (10 g) minced garlic

1 tablespoon (7 g) smoked paprika

1 teaspoon sea salt

1 teaspoon ground cumin

2 dried bay leaves

1½ quarts (1.4 L) chicken broth, home-made (page 242) or store-bought

1 cup (235 ml) coconut milk

1 To make the shrimp, put the shrimp in a bowl and sprinkle with a few generous pinches of salt and the juice from half of the lime. Let them sit while you prep the soup.

2 To make the soup, char the bell peppers and jalapeño by either grilling them over high heat or putting them directly onto the grates over the gas burners on your stove turned to medium heat. If you don't have a grill or a gas stove, you can put them under the oven broiler (top rack), but it takes about twice as long. Use tongs to turn them so most of the peppers have blistered black spots. This takes 10–15 minutes.

3 Meanwhile, put the 1 tablespoon (15 ml) of ghee in the pressure cooker pot. Turn the cooker to the high sauté setting. Add the onion, carrots, and celery to the pot and cook for a few minutes until the onions soften. Add the garlic and then turn off the cooker.

4 Add the smoked paprika, salt, cumin, bay leaves, and chicken broth to the pot.

5 When the peppers are finished charring, cover them with aluminum foil or plastic wrap so they can steam for a few minutes (this makes them much easier to peel). Peel off some of the blackened skin (You don't need to remove all the skin, so don't stress.) Cut off the stems and remove the large bunch of seeds; discard the stems and seeds. Put the peppers in the cooker.

6 Put the lid on the cooker and close the steam valve. Set the cooker to high pressure for 5 minutes. Let the cooker release pressure naturally for 10 minutes before releasing the rest of the pressure manually.

7 When the soup starts to depressurize, put the ¼ cup (60 ml) ghee into a skillet over medium-high heat. When it is hot, add the 1 teaspoon of garlic and a pinch of red pepper flakes to the ghee and cook for about 30 seconds, stirring constantly. Add the shrimp to the skillet and cook just until they turn pink all over—this should only take 5 minutes

or so. (Don't overcook them or they'll be rubbery.) Remove from the heat and keep the shrimp and juices warm until ready to serve.

8 When the soup is finished, remove the bay leaves and discard them and then blend the soup with an immersion blender (or in batches using a countertop blender). Stir in the coconut milk. Taste and add some salt or juice from the other ½ lime if you think it needs it.

9 Ladle the soup into bowls and add a few pieces of shrimp and a drizzle of garlic ghee (from the skillet).

10 Serve.

Buffalo Ranch Chicken Chowder

I feel like I was late to the "buffalo everything" craze, but I'm making up for it with recipes like this chowder. Ranch and wing sauce go so well together, the ranch cooling the spiciness of the sauce and adding creaminess. Using ranch dressing as a drizzle for a soup might seem odd, but it's the perfect finishing touch to this spicy, buffalo-style soup.

Prep time 20 minutes

Pressure time 10 minutes + 10 minutes natural release

Serves 8

1½ pounds (680 g) chicken breasts or thighs, cut into 1-inch (2.5 cm) pieces

1 teaspoon Chorizo Seasoning (page 243)

3 tablespoons (45 ml) ghee (page 234)

One 15-ounce (425 g) can crushed tomatoes

1 cup (160 g) diced onion

2 medium carrots, peeled and diced

2 celery stalks, diced

1 pound (455 g) potatoes (red or sweet), cut into ½-inch (1.3 cm) pieces

1 tablespoon (10 g) minced garlic

½ cup (120 ml) cayenne pepper sauce

1½ cups (355 ml) chicken broth, homemade (page 242) or store-bought

One 13-ounce (370 g) can coconut milk

3 tablespoons (23 g) tapioca flour

Paleo-Friendly Ranch Dressing (page 237), for serving

Chopped fresh parsley, for serving

1 Place the chicken on a large plate and sprinkle with the Chorizo Seasoning.

2 Turn the cooker to the high sauté setting. Add the ghee to the pot and when it has preheated, sear the chicken pieces on each side until golden brown.

3 Add the tomatoes, onion, carrots, celery, potatoes, garlic, cayenne pepper sauce, and chicken broth to the pot.

4 Close the lid and the steam valve and set the cooker to high pressure for 10 minutes. Let the cooker release pressure naturally for 10 minutes and then manually release the rest of the pressure.

5 Whisk the coconut milk with the tapioca flour and stir the mixture into the chowder. Turn the cooker to medium sauté and cook until bubbly and thickened. Turn off the cooker.

6 Serve the chowder with a drizzle of Paleo-Friendly Ranch Dressing and a sprinkle of fresh parsley.

Chipotle Sweet Potato Chowder with Bacon

Here's another creamy chowder with a punch of spice—this time in the form of chipotle peppers. I adore chipotle peppers and their smoky heat. They're a perfect complement to the sweet potatoes and salty bacon in this chowder.

Prep time 30 minutes

Pressure time 10 minutes + 10 minutes natural release

Serves 6

8 slices of thick-cut, uncured, nitrate-free bacon, cut into ½-inch (1.3 cm) pieces

1 large onion, diced

2–2½ pounds (900–1135 g) sweet potatoes, peeled and cut into ½-inch (1.3 cm) pieces

1 chipotle pepper, from a can of chipotle peppers in adobo sauce, minced

2 teaspoons minced garlic

1 teaspoons sea salt

½ teaspoon dried thyme

½ teaspoon dried marjoram

3 cups (700 ml) chicken broth, homemade (page 242) or store-bought

One 13-ounce (370 g) can full-fat coconut milk

3 tablespoons (23 g) tapioca flour

3 scallions, trimmed and thinly sliced

1 tablespoon (15 ml) freshly squeezed lime juice

1 Turn the cooker to the high sauté setting. Add the bacon to the pot and cook until crispy, stirring often, 15–20 minutes. Remove the bacon and set aside.

2 Add the onion and cook until golden brown and caramelized, stirring often, about 10 minutes.

3 Add the sweet potatoes, chipotle pepper, garlic, salt, thyme, marjoram, and chicken broth.

4 Close the lid and the steam valve and set the cooker to high pressure for 10 minutes. Allow the pressure to release naturally for 10 minutes and then release the rest of the pressure manually, if you wish. Remove the lid.

5 Turn the cooker to the high sauté setting. Whisk the coconut milk with the tapioca flour and stir it into the soup. Cook until bubbly and thickened, about 5 minutes.

6 Stir the reserved bacon, scallions, and lime juice into the soup. Taste and add more salt or lime juice as needed.

7 Serve.

Simple Creamy Potato Chowder

This soup is just cozy. Like the name says, it's simple and creamy and takes potato chowder to its basic form without any extra frills. Don't get me wrong—I love frills, but sometimes I'm in the mood for simplicity and this soup fills that craving.

Prep time 10 minutes

Pressure time 10 minutes + 10 minutes natural release

Serves 8

3 pounds (1.4 kg) red, Yukon, or russet potatoes, cut into ½-inch (1.3 cm) cubes

1 tablespoon (5 g) dried minced onion

2 teaspoons sea salt

1 quart (946 ml) chicken broth, homemade (page 242) or store-bought

2 cups (475 ml) unsweetened almond milk, divided

3 tablespoons (23 g) tapioca flour

½ cup (120 ml) ghee (page 234) or grass-fed butter

1 cup (100 g) thinly sliced scallions or (48 g) chives, for serving

Freshly ground black pepper, for serving

1 Add the potatoes, dried minced onion, salt, chicken broth, and 1 cup (235 ml) of the almond milk to the pot.

2 Close the lid and the steam valve and set your cooker to high pressure for 10 minutes. Allow the cooker to release the pressure on its own for at least 10 minutes and then you can release the rest of the pressure manually.

3 Ladle 3-4 cups (700-946 ml) of the soup into a blender and blend until smooth. Pour the blended soup back into the pot with the rest of the soup.

4 Set the cooker to medium sauté. Whisk together the remaining 1 cup (235 ml) of almond milk and the tapioca flour. Stir the mixture into the soup along with the ghee.

5 Let the soup simmer for a few minutes until it has thickened, stirring often.

6 Taste and add more salt if needed. Serve with a sprinkle of scallions and a pinch or two of freshly ground black pepper.

Note: You could add cooked, chopped bacon or ham at the end as well.

Vegetarian Paleo Chili

Occasionally, readers ask me for meatless recipes, and it's often hard to create hearty recipes that are both vegetarian and paleo-friendly. This chili fills both needs. And if you're craving some extra protein, try adding a fried or poached egg on top.

Prep time 20 minutes

Pressure time 5 minutes + 5 minutes natural release

Serves 6

2 tablespoons (28 ml) avocado or (28 g) coconut oil

1 medium red onion, chopped

1 green bell pepper, seeded and chopped

1 medium sweet potato, peeled and cut into ½-inch (1.3 cm) pieces

3 cups (420 g) cubed butternut squash, cut into ½-inch (1.3 cm) pieces

1 tablespoon (10 g) minced garlic

1 tablespoon (8 g) chili powder

2 teaspoons unsweetened cocoa powder

1 teaspoon ground cumin

1 teaspoon sea salt

¼–1 teaspoon cayenne pepper (depending on how spicy you want it)

¼ teaspoon ground cinnamon

One 28-ounce (785 g) can diced tomatoes, undrained

2 cups (475 ml) vegetable broth

½ cup (8 g) chopped fresh cilantro

Poached or fried eggs, for serving (optional)

1 Turn the cooker to high sauté and add the oil. Add the onion and bell pepper to the pot. Cook for 4–5 minutes until the onions are soft and translucent.

2 Add the rest of the ingredients (except the cilantro and eggs) and stir. Cover the cooker, close the steam valve, and set the cooker to high pressure for 5 minutes. Let the cooker release pressure naturally for 5 minutes and then release the rest of the pressure manually.

3 Stir in the cilantro and taste, adding more salt if needed.

4 Ladle into bowls and add a poached egg on top if you wish. (It's really great that way.)

5 Serve.

Turkey, Bacon, and Avocado Chili

This is a lighter, "California-style" chili, and I love the chunks of creamy avocado throughout. The avocado fills the need I have to add a creamy component to chili without reaching for sour cream. And bacon makes everything more interesting, no?

Prep time 20 minutes

Pressure time 5 minutes +
5 minutes natural release

Serves 6

10 ounces (280 g) uncooked bacon, chopped

1 pound (455 g) ground turkey or chicken

1 cup (160 g) diced sweet onion

6 ounces (170 g) brown mushrooms, diced

1 bell pepper, any color, seeded and diced

3 tablespoons (19 g) Chorizo Seasoning (page 243)

1 tablespoon (10 g) minced garlic

1 teaspoon sea salt

One 15-ounce (425 g) can diced tomatoes

One 15-ounce (425 g) can tomato sauce

1 lime

2 scallions, trimmed and thinly sliced

2 avocados, peeled, pitted, and diced

Hot sauce, for serving

1 Turn the cooker to the medium sauté setting. Add the chopped bacon and cook, stirring often, until crispy. (You can use this time to prep the other ingredients, if you like.) Using a slotted spoon, transfer the bacon to a folded paper towel to drain off some of the grease. Leave the bacon drippings in the pot.

2 To the pot, add the ground turkey and the onion. Cook, stirring often and breaking the meat into bits, until it is fully cooked and the onion is soft and translucent.

3 Add the mushrooms, bell pepper, Chorizo Seasoning, garlic, salt, diced tomatoes, and tomato sauce. Stir well.

4 Close the lid and the steam valve. Set it to high pressure for 5 minutes. Let the cooker release pressure on its own for at least 5 minutes before releasing the rest manually.

5 Stir in the juice from ½ of the lime, scallions, avocados, and reserved bacon. Taste and add additional lime juice or salt, if needed.

6 Serve with a shake or two of hot sauce, if you like.

Chipotle Pork and Sweet Potato Chili

Pork is a fun, unexpected addition to chili and it plays well with the sweetness from the sweet potatoes and the spice of chipotle. I like to buy a whole pork loin, chop it into cubes, and freeze it in 1-pound (455 g) portions so I can easily use it in recipes like this.

Prep time 20 minutes

Pressure time 15 minutes + 10 minutes natural release

Serves 6

2 teaspoons (6 g) steak seasoning, divided

1 pound (455 g) pork loin, cut into ½–1 inch (1.3–2.5 cm) pieces

2 tablespoons (28 ml) avocado oil, divided

1 large sweet onion, diced

1 bell pepper, seeded and diced

One 4-ounce (115 g) can diced green chiles

1 chipotle pepper, from a can of chipotles in adobo sauce, seeded (optional) and minced

2 teaspoons minced garlic

1 pound (455 g) sweet potatoes, cut into 1-inch (2.5 cm) pieces

1 tablespoon (16 g) tomato paste

One 15-ounce (425 g) can crushed tomatoes

2 tablespoons (28 ml) apple cider vinegar

1 tablespoon (8 g) chili powder

1 cup (235 ml) chicken broth, homemade (page 242) or store-bought

½ cup (8 g) chopped fresh cilantro

1 Sprinkle 1 teaspoon of the steak seasoning on the pork.

2 Turn the cooker to high sauté and add 1 tablespoon (15 ml) of the avocado oil to the pot. When the pot has preheated, add half of the pork to the pot. Sear on one side for 3–4 minutes to form a golden crust and then toss it around and cook for another couple of minutes. The pieces don't have to be cooked all the way through at this point. Repeat with the remaining 1 tablespoon (15 ml) of avocado oil and pork.

3 Add the reserved pork back to the pot and then add the onion, bell pepper, diced green chiles, and chipotle pepper. Stir and cook for 2–3 minutes. Turn the cooker off.

4 Add the rest of the ingredients (except the cilantro). Be sure to include the remaining 1 teaspoon of steak seasoning. Stir well.

5 Close the lid and the steam valve. Set the cooker to high pressure for 15 minutes. Let it release the pressure on its own for about 10 minutes before manually releasing the rest of the pressure.

6 Open the cooker and stir in the cilantro. Taste and add more salt, if needed.

7 Serve.

Hearty Steak and Potato Chili

My friends, this is the chili to end all chili. It's hearty and rich and flavorful with chunks of potato throughout to lighten it up a bit. This has been one of the most popular recipes on my website for years, and many of my readers have entered (and won!) chili competitions with it. I decided it needed to have a spot in this book, so I made it pressure cooker friendly—just for you.

Prep time 30 minutes
Pressure time 20 minutes + 15 minutes natural release
Serves 8–10

Note: Butternut squash cubes work well in place of the potatoes if you're avoiding white potatoes.

3 tablespoons (24 g) chili powder
1 tablespoon (7 g) ground cumin
2 teaspoons sea salt
1½ teaspoons dried oregano
1 teaspoon black pepper
½ teaspoon ground cinnamon
¼ teaspoon cayenne pepper
2½–3 pounds (1.1–1.4 kg) sirloin steak or stew meat, cut into 1-inch (2.5 cm) pieces
3 tablespoons (45 ml) avocado oil, divided
3 cups (480 g) diced sweet onion (about 1½ large)
1½ cups (180 g) diced celery (about 4 stalks)

1 tablespoon (10 g) minced garlic
1 cup (235 ml) beef broth, homemade (page 242) or store-bought
2 tablespoons (32 g) tomato paste
1 ounce (28 g) semisweet or 70% cacao dark chocolate
One 28-ounce (785 g) can crushed tomatoes
1½ pounds (680 g) red or Yukon gold potatoes, cut into 1-inch (2.5 cm) pieces
½ cup (8 g) chopped fresh cilantro
½ cup (30 g) chopped fresh parsley

Garnishes
thinly sliced scallions, hot sauce, and diced avocado

1 Combine the chili powder, cumin, salt, oregano, black pepper, cinnamon, and cayenne pepper in a large bowl. Add the beef to the bowl and toss to coat the beef in the spices.

2 Put 1 tablespoon (15 ml) of the avocado oil in the pot. Set the cooker to high sauté. When it is preheated, add one-third of the beef and sear for 3–4 minutes, flipping the pieces around once. Transfer the beef to a large plate. Repeat in two more batches with the remaining 2 tablespoons (28 ml) of avocado oil and beef and then transfer the beef to the plate.

3 Add the onion, celery, and garlic to the pot and cook for 2–3 minutes until the vegetables have softened. If the juices from the vegetables aren't enough to loosen the bits stuck to the bottom of the pot, add ¼ cup (60 ml) of the beef broth to help it along.

4 Add the rest of the beef broth along with the reserved beef, tomato paste, chocolate, crushed tomatoes, and potatoes. Give it a good stir.

5 Close the lid and the steam valve. Set the cooker to high pressure for 20 minutes. Let the cooker release pressure naturally for 15 minutes and then release any remaining pressure manually.

6 Stir in the cilantro and parsley and taste, adding a little salt if needed.

7 Serve the chili with the preferred garnishes.

3

MEAL PREP SHORTCUT RECIPES

Weekend meal prepping has become popular among CrossFit enthusiasts and paleo fanatics—and for good reason. Making big batches of prepared dishes or shredded meat ahead of time allows you to have a head start on dinner later in the week—or a month or two down the road. In this chapter, I give you basic recipes for shredded chicken, beef, and pork and almost a dozen recipes to create quick, easy meals from those made-ahead portions of protein. So, dinner shortcuts.

Recipes

Basic Shredded Chicken

Everyone needs a basic shredded chicken recipe and this is mine. I like my shredded chicken to be delicious enough to eat on its own, yet simply seasoned so it can take on other seasoning and flavors when I use it in other recipes. This one freezes well, so you can pull it out and use it in other recipes—like the ones listed in the next few pages.

Prep time 15 minutes

Pressure time 30 minutes + 15 minutes natural release

Makes 7-8 cups (980-1120 g) shredded meat

1 lemon

5 pounds (2.3 kg) boneless, skinless chicken breasts or thighs

1½ teaspoons sea salt

1 teaspoon granulated garlic

½ teaspoon black pepper

2-3 tablespoons (28-45 ml) avocado oil

½ cup (120 ml) chicken broth, homemade (page 242) or store-bought, or water

1 Squeeze the juice from the lemon over the chicken. Sprinkle the salt, garlic, and pepper over the chicken, coating each side.

2 Turn the cooker to the high sauté setting and add the avocado oil. Sear 2-3 pieces of chicken at a time until the sides are golden brown, 2-3 minutes on each side. You'll probably need to do this in multiple batches.

3 When all of the chicken has been seared, place them in the pot, add the chicken broth, and set it to high pressure for 30 minutes. Let the cooker release pressure naturally for 15 minutes and then release the rest of the pressure manually.

4 Remove the chicken from the pot, shred it and then return it to the pot to soak up some of the pot juices and flavor.

5 Store the chicken with its juices until ready to use—either chilled or frozen.

Note: Searing is optional, but I think it adds enough flavor to make it worth it.

Quick Teriyaki Chicken Stir-Fry

Using shredded chicken in a stir-fry may seem unorthodox, but I quite like how the tender shreds mix with the vegetables and absorb the stir-fry sauce.

Prep time 5 minutes
Cook time 10 minutes
Serves 6

2 tablespoons (28 ml) sesame oil

1 tablespoon (10 g) finely grated ginger

1 teaspoon minced garlic

1 pound (455 g) bag frozen stir-fry vegetables

1½ cups (210 g) leftover Basic Shredded Chicken (page 78)

2 tablespoons (28 ml) rice vinegar

1 cup (235 ml) Paleo Teriyaki Sauce (page 236)

3 scallions, thinly sliced

Roasted Cauliflower Rice (page 200), for serving

1 Heat the sesame oil in a large skillet over high heat. Add the ginger and garlic; cook for 1 minute. Add the frozen vegetables and cover to steam them for 4-5 minutes.

2 When the vegetables are thawed out, uncover and add the shredded chicken, vinegar, and Paleo Teriyaki Sauce. Toss to combine and cook until everything is heated through and the juices from the pan have reduced some, about 3 minutes.

3 Sprinkle the scallions over the stir-fry and serve over Roasted Cauliflower Rice.

Note: If you prep the cauliflower rice and put it in the oven before beginning the stir-fry, they should both be done around the same time.

Honey-Dijon Chicken and Apple Salad

This is my favorite chicken salad. Apples and celery give the salad some crunch and the honey-Dijon dressing is the perfect blend of sweet and tangy. If I have some leftover shredded chicken, it usually ends up in this salad and as my lunch for the next few days.

Prep time 15 minutes
Serves 6

3½–4 cups (490–560 g) leftover Basic Shredded Chicken (page 78), drained

1 cup (150 g) diced apple

1 celery stalk, diced

1 scallion, thinly sliced

1 cup toasted nuts ([100 g] pecans, [100 g] walnuts, [140 g] cashews, or [92 g] sliced almonds)

1 cup (225 g) Paleo-Friendly Mayonnaise (page 230)

1 tablespoon (15 g) Dijon mustard

1 tablespoon (20 g) honey

Sea salt (optional)

Lettuce leaves, for serving

1 If the leftover shredded chicken has a lot of gelatinized juices in it, put it in a skillet and cook it over medium heat until the juices melt and can be drained.

2 Place the chicken in a large bowl. Add the apple, celery, scallion, and nuts.

3 Whisk together the Paleo-friendly Mayonnaise, mustard, and honey. Pour the dressing over the salad and fold gently to combine. Taste and add a few pinches of salt, if necessary.

4 Serve the chicken salad alone or in a lettuce cup.

Easy Coconut-Lime Chicken Curry

This simple curry was originally a vegetarian curry on my website, but swapping out the chickpeas for chicken was an easy way to keep this meal under 30 minutes and make it paleo-friendly.

Prep time 10 minutes
Cook time 15 minutes
Serves 8

2 tablespoons (28 ml) ghee (page 234) or coconut oil

1 cup (160 g) chopped sweet onion

4 large carrots, peeled and cut into ½-inch (1.3 cm) pieces

1 small head of cauliflower, cut into 1-inch (2.5 cm) florets

3 tablespoons (24 g) Madras curry powder

Pinch of crushed red pepper flakes

1 teaspoon sea salt

1½ cups (355 ml) chicken broth, homemade (page 242) or store-bought

3–4 cups (420–560 g) leftover Basic Shredded Chicken (page 78)

One 13-ounce (370 g) can full-fat coconut milk

Zest and juice of 1 large juicy lime

2 teaspoons garam masala

2 tablespoons (12 g) chopped fresh mint

Roasted Cauliflower Rice (page 200) or cooked jasmine rice, for serving

Sriracha or Asian chili paste, for serving (optional)

1 Heat the ghee in a large skillet over medium-high heat. Add the onion, carrots, and cauliflower. Cook for 2–3 minutes.

2 Add the curry powder, red pepper flakes, and salt. Cook for another minute or so.

3 Add the chicken broth and shredded chicken. Bring to a simmer. Reduce the heat to medium-low and cover. Let it simmer gently for 10 minutes until the carrots are mostly cooked.

4 Add the coconut milk, lime zest, and lime juice and let it cook for 5 more minutes until the carrots are tender. Add the garam masala and fresh mint.

5 Serve the curry over Roasted Cauliflower Rice with some sriracha, if desired.

Basic Shredded Beef

I get just as excited about finding a package of grass-fed shredded beef in my freezer (when I thought we had eaten it all) as I do when I find a $50 bill in the pocket of my coat. Prepped shredded beef is such a treasure and so versatile.

Prep time 10 minutes

Pressure time 80 minutes + 15 minutes natural release

Makes 6–7 cups (1.2–1.4 kg) shredded meat

One 3- to 4-pound (1.4–1.8 kg) beef roast

1 teaspoon sea salt

1 teaspoon granulated garlic

1 teaspoon onion powder

½ teaspoon black pepper

2 tablespoons (28 ml) ghee (page 234), coconut oil, or avocado oil

⅓ cup (80 ml) coconut aminos

⅓ cup (80 ml) beef broth, homemade (page 242) or store-bought

1 Cut the beef roast into 3 or 4 pieces.

2 Combine the salt, garlic, onion powder, and pepper in a small bowl. Rub the spice blend on the pieces of roast.

3 Turn the cooker on the high sauté setting and add the ghee. When it has preheated, sear the roast pieces on a couple of sides, each side for about 5 minutes undisturbed, until it forms a golden brown crust.

4 Add the coconut aminos and beef broth to the pot.

5 Close the lid and the steam valve. Set the cooker to high pressure for 80 minutes. Let the cooker release all of the pressure naturally or for at least for 15 minutes before releasing it manually.

6 Remove the pieces of beef from the pot and shred them, discarding any large pieces of fat or connective tissue. Return the shredded beef to the pot with the juices.

7 At this point, you can eat it as it or divide it into containers to chill or freeze and use in any of the quick shredded beef recipes that follow.

Shredded Beef with Caramelized Onions and Mushrooms

This recipe, full of hearty, rich flavors, is perfect for a chilly winter weeknight. Just turn on your favorite Netflix show and you'll have this whipped up and ready to eat before it's over.

Prep time 5 minutes
Cook time About 25 minutes
Serves 4

2 tablespoons (28 ml) ghee (page 234) or avocado oil, divided

1 large onion, thinly sliced

Sea salt

12 ounces (340 g) brown mushrooms, sliced

2 sprigs of fresh rosemary or ¼ teaspoon dried rosemary

2 sprigs of fresh thyme or ⅛ teaspoon dried thyme

2½–3 cups (500–600 g) leftover Basic Shredded Beef (page 83), with juices

½ cup (120 ml) beef broth, homemade (page 242) or store-bought (optional)

1 tablespoon (15 ml) red wine vinegar

⅓ cup (80 ml) coconut cream (optional)

1 Heat the ghee in a large skillet over medium-high heat. Add the onion with a couple generous pinches of salt. Cook, tossing the onions around frequently, until they have softened and are translucent, 5–7 minutes. Cover, reduce the heat to medium-low, and cook for another 5–7 minutes until the onions are light golden brown.

2 Add the mushrooms and fresh herbs. Turn the heat up slightly, to medium, and cook, covered, for 5 minutes.

3 Remove the lid and continue to cook until the mushrooms are very tender and the onions are a darker golden brown.

4 Add the shredded beef with its juices and cook for a few minutes until everything is heated through. Remove the herb stems and discard. If there isn't enough sauce from the beef, add the beef broth. Add the vinegar as well.

5 If you'd like this to be creamy, stir in the coconut cream and cook for another minute or two.

6 Serve with your desired side dish.

Recommended sides: Roasted Cauliflower Rice (page 200), squash noodles, or potatoes

Chipotle Shredded Taco Beef

This taco meat comes together so quickly you'll never be caught unprepared on a Taco Tuesday again as long as your freezer is stocked with shredded beef Or chicken. Or pork. You could use any type of shredded meat in this!

Prep time 5 minutes
Cook time 10 minutes
Serves 6

1 tablespoon (15 ml) avocado oil

½ large onion, diced

1 chipotle pepper, from a can of chipotle peppers in adobo sauce, minced

1 teaspoon minced garlic

1 teaspoon chili powder

½ teaspoon ground cumin

1 tablespoon (16 g) tomato paste

3 cups (600 g) leftover Basic Shredded Beef (page 83), with juices

½ cup (120 ml) beef broth, homemade (page 242) or store-bought, or water (optional)

1 lime

1 Heat the avocado oil in a large skillet over medium-high heat. Add the onion and cook for 5–8 minutes until it is soft and translucent.

2 Add the chipotle pepper, garlic, chili powder, cumin, tomato paste, and shredded beef. If you feel it needs to be saucier, add the beef broth or water.

3 Stir everything together well and reduce the heat to medium-low. Simmer for about 10 minutes to warm everything through.

4 Add the juice from half of the lime, reserving the rest for garnish.

5 Serve with your desired sides.

Recommended uses: In a taco salad, over Roasted Cauliflower Rice (page 200), or on a Whole Steamed Sweet Potato (page 183)

Note: Chipotle peppers add a wonderful smoky flavor to Tex-Mex type recipes, but can be very spicy. Remove the seeds from the pepper if you want to tone it down a bit.

Sloppy Joe–Stuffed Sweet Potatoes

Sloppy Joes have been a staple in my dinner rotation for most of my life, and this was the first time I made them with shredded beef instead of ground beef. I've gotta say, I might actually like them better this way. Because it was already seasoned, the leftover shredded beef added more flavor.

Prep time 5 minutes
Cook time 10 minutes
(plus cooking time for potatoes)
Serves 6

2-2½ pounds (900-1135 g) Whole Steamed Potatoes, white or sweet (page 183)

3 cups (600 g) leftover Basic Shredded Beef (page 83)

One 15-ounce (425 g) can tomato sauce

3 tablespoons (33 g) yellow mustard

2 tablespoons (40 g) honey or (30 g) Date Paste (page 232)

1 tablespoon (5 g) dried minced onion

1½ teaspoons chili powder

¾ teaspoon ground or rubbed sage

⅓ cup (80 ml) water (optional)

Sea salt (optional)

Diced pickles, for serving

Paleo-Friendly Ranch Dressing (page 237), for serving

1 Start the potatoes first using the instructions on page 183.

2 Put the shredded beef into a large skillet with the tomato sauce, mustard, honey, dried onion, chili powder, and sage. Cook over medium heat until everything is heated through and bubbly. If the sauce is too thick, add the water. Taste and add a little salt, if necessary. The leftover beef may have enough salt already.

3 Serve the Sloppy Joe mixture on a halved steamed potato and top with diced pickles and a drizzle of Paleo-friendly Ranch Dressing.

Basic Shredded Pork

Typically, the shredded pork in our house eventually turns into carnitas, but luckily, pork is super versatile and can take on as many flavors as you can toss with it. Having a few packages of this in your freezer will ensure quick meals for weeks to come.

Prep time 15 minutes

Pressure time 60 minutes + 15 minutes natural release

Makes 7–8 cups (1.4–1.6 kg) meat

One 4- to 5-pound (1.8–2.3 kg) pork shoulder roast, bone-in or boneless

2 teaspoons sea salt

1 teaspoon black pepper

2 tablespoons (28 ml) bacon drippings or avocado oil

½ cup (120 ml) chicken broth, homemade (page 242) or store-bought, or vegetable broth

½ large onion, thinly sliced

2 teaspoons minced garlic

3 dried bay leaves

1 Cut the roast into 4 roughly equal pieces. Rub the salt and pepper all over the pork.

2 Turn the cooker to the high sauté setting and add the bacon drippings. When it has preheated, sear the pork (if you can fit them all; if not, then sear it in batches) until a golden crust forms on a couple of the sides.

3 Pour in the broth to deglaze the pot. Add the onion, garlic, and bay leaves on top of the pork.

4 Close the lid and the steam valve. Set the cooker to high pressure for 60 minutes. Allow the cooker to release the pressure naturally for at least 15 minutes before manually releasing the rest of the pressure.

5 Remove the bay leaves from the pot. Remove the pork, shred it with two forks, and return it to the pot with the juices.

6 Divide the pork and juices into lidded containers to store chilled or frozen.

Shortcut Pork Carnitas with Watermelon-Cucumber Salsa

The only thing better than pork carnitas is really fast pork carnitas with fruit salsa. The watermelon is an unexpected addition, but adds a punch of sweet, summery flavor.

Prep time About 30 minutes
Serves 6

3-4 cups (600-800 g) leftover Basic Shredded Pork (page 88), drained of cooking juices

Juice from ½ large orange (about ¼ cup [60 ml])

3 limes, divided

1 teaspoon minced garlic

Pinch of ground cumin

½ cup (8 g) chopped fresh cilantro

Lettuce leaves or paleo tortillas, for serving

For the salsa:

2 cups (300 g) quartered cherry or grape tomatoes

1½ cups (225 g) diced watermelon (cut into ½-inch [1.3 cm] pieces)

¾ cup (101 g) diced cucumber (cut into ½-inch [1.3 cm] pieces)

¾ cup (120 g) diced sweet onion

Juice from 1 lime (about 2 tablespoons [28 ml])

1½ tablespoons (9 g) chopped fresh mint

1½ tablespoons (1.5 g) chopped fresh cilantro

¼ teaspoon chili powder

A generous pinch or two of sea salt

1½–2 teaspoons hot sauce (optional)

1 Preheat your oven broiler and place an oven rack 6 inches (15 cm) from the heating element.

2 Spread the shredded pork out on a rimmed baking sheet. Mix together the orange juice, the juice from 1 of the limes, garlic, cumin, and cilantro. Pour it over the pork and toss to combine.

3 Broil the pork for 12–15 minutes, stirring a couple of times during cooking, until the juices have cooked off and the pork has crispy edges scattered throughout.

4 To make the salsa, combine all of the salsa ingredients in a medium bowl. Stir well.

5 Remove the pork from the oven and sprinkle the ½ cup (8 g) of cilantro over the top. Cut the remaining 2 limes into wedges.

6 Serve the pork in either lettuce leaves or paleo tortillas with the salsa and lime wedges alongside.

Note: If the cooking juices have gelatinized, heat the meat and juices in a skillet for a minute or two to let the juices liquefy and then drain them off.

Crispy Za'atar Pork Salad with Tahini Dressing

Have you ever had za'atar seasoning? It's a Middle Eastern blend that is found in some well-stocked grocery stores. If you can't find za'atar, you can definitely make your own. Just do a quick Internet search and find a recipe. One of the primary spices is sumac, which might be hard to track down, but is readily available online. What did we ever do before the Internet?

Prep time 15 minutes
Serves 4

2 tablespoons (28 ml) avocado oil

2 cups (400 g) leftover Basic Shredded Pork (page 88) drained if possible

1 teaspoon za'atar seasoning

1 large head of green leaf lettuce, chopped

1 English cucumber, diced

Toasted sesame seeds, for garnish

Chopped fresh parsley, for garnish

For the dressing:

¼ cup (60 ml) freshly squeezed lemon juice

1 tablespoon (15 g) tahini

½ clove garlic, minced

1 teaspoon honey

6 tablespoons (90 ml) avocado oil

Pinch of sea salt and black pepper

1 Put the avocado oil in a large skillet over medium-high heat. Add the shredded pork to the skillet with as little of the pork juices as possible. Add the za'atar seasoning. Stir it frequently, breaking the pork into shreds, until the juices have cooked off and the pork has become browned and crispy on the edges, about 15 minutes.

2 To make the dressing, whisk together the lemon juice, tahini, garlic, and honey. Continue to whisk while drizzling in the avocado oil. Add a pinch of salt and pepper. Taste and adjust the seasonings.

3 Assemble the salads by placing a bed of salad greens in each bowl and topping with some pork, diced cucumber, and a drizzle of dressing. Top with toasted sesame seeds and fresh parsley.

Note: You can also use my Middle Eastern Seasoning (page 245) in place of the za'atar if you wish.

BBQ Pork–Stuffed Peppers with Nacho Cheeze Sauce

This quick prep recipe is heavily dependent on having some key items prepped ahead of time. Even if you don't have the BBQ or cheeze sauces made, you can whip those up in about 15 minutes (assuming you've soaked your cashews), still making this a quick and easy meal.

Prep time 10 minutes
Pressure time 8 minutes
Serves 4

4 bell peppers, any color (choose ones that can stand on their own)

2 cups (400 g) leftover Basic Shredded Pork (page 88)

1 cup (235 ml) Smoky Maple BBQ Sauce (page 239)

1 recipe Spicy Nacho Sauce (page 240)

1 Put 1 cup (235 ml) of water and the wire rack in the pot.

2 Cut the tops off of the peppers and clean out the seeds from the insides.

3 Mix the shredded pork with the Smoky Maple BBQ Sauce. Put ½ cup (120 ml) of the BBQ pork inside each hollowed-out pepper.

4 Place the peppers on the wire rack. Close the lid and the steam valve. Set the cooker to high pressure for 8 minutes. Release the pressure manually and remove the peppers from the pot.

5 Warm the Spicy Nacho Sauce, if necessary. Serve the peppers with a few spoonfuls of warm sauce.

Soft- or Hard-Cooked Eggs

One of the first things I made in my pressure cooker was a batch of hard-cooked eggs. I couldn't believe how easy it was to have perfectly cooked, easy-to-peel eggs without babysitting (and often forgetting) a pan on the stove!

I've found that cooking times for eggs vary depending on where you live. Four minutes is perfect for me, whereas 5 minutes is perfect for a lot of other people who have tested them out. Try 5 minutes for hard-cooked eggs and adjust the cooking time for subsequent batches as needed. You'll find your gray-ring-free cooking time, and you'll never go back to boiling water on the stove again.

Prep time 2 minutes
Pressure time 2–5 minutes
Makes up to 14 eggs

Any number of large, uncooked eggs

1 Add a cup (235 ml) of water to your pot and place the wire rack on the bottom. Lay as many large, uncooked eggs as will fit on the wire rack in a single layer. I can usually get 14 at the most.

2 Close the lid and the steam valve and set the cooker to high pressure for 2, 3, or 4 minutes— 2 minutes if you want soft-cooked eggs with runny yolks, 3 minutes if you want slightly soft yolks, and 4 minutes if you want perfectly hard-cooked yolks.

3 Prepare a bowl of ice water while the eggs are cooking.

4 When they're finished, release the pressure manually. Open the lid and immediately transfer the eggs to the ice bath.

5 When they are cool enough to handle, go ahead and peel them. I've found that they're much easier to peel when they've cooled off all the way.

Smoked Salmon Egg Salad with Fresh Dill

This is a fresh, springy take on egg salad. I just adore fresh dill—especially with smoked salmon. If you happen to have some "Everything But the Bagel" seasoning that's becoming popular online, it's fabulous on this salad. I included a quick, simplified version for you in the recipe, using sesame seeds, dried minced onion, and dried minced garlic, but if you'd like to make the full version yourself, you can find my recipe on perrysplate.com.

Prep time 15 minutes
Serves 6

12 Hard-Cooked Eggs (page 93)

⅓ cup (75 g) Paleo-Friendly Mayonnaise (page 230)

2 tablespoons (28 ml) freshly squeezed lemon juice

1 cup (143 g) chopped pickles

3 tablespoons (12 g) chopped fresh dill

4–5 ounces (115-140 g) smoked salmon, crumbled

1 teaspoon toasted sesame seeds

1 teaspoon dried minced onion

½ teaspoon dried minced garlic or ¼ teaspoon garlic powder

¼ teaspoon sea salt

1 Peel and dice the eggs. Place them in a large bowl.

2 Add the Paleo-Friendly Mayonnaise and lemon juice. Smash everything together with a fork until creamy and well mixed.

3 Stir in the pickles, dill, salmon, sesame seeds, dried onion, dried garlic, and salt. Taste and add more salt if needed.

4 Serve alone or spoon into lettuce cups.

Poached Eggs

Poaching eggs in a pressure cooker was a game changer for me! I've always been poaching impaired when it came to eggs. They always turned out messy and more white was left in the saucepan than on my plate. Invest in a few silicone egg-poaching cups (I found mine on Amazon!) and you'll always have perfectly formed, perfectly cooked poached eggs.

Prep time 5 minutes

Pressure time 2-3 minutes

Makes up to 5 eggs, depending on the size of your poaching cups

Up to 5 large, uncooked eggs

1 Add a cup (235 ml) of water to your pot and place the wire rack on the bottom.

2 Crack one egg into each poaching cup and carefully place the cups on the wire rack.

3 Close the lid and the steam valve and set the cooker to high pressure for 2 or 3 minutes. Two minutes will give you a very runny yolk and 3 minutes will give you a slightly more cooked, "jelly" yolk.

4 When the pressure cooking time is over, release the pressure manually and remove the cups from the cooker.

5 To remove the eggs from the cups, use a large spoon to loosen it from the edges of the cup and scoop it out from the bottom. (Like you'd remove an avocado half from the skin.)

Note: You can find silicon egg poaching cups in kitchen retail stores and online.

BLT Egg Salad

If putting a fried egg on a BLT makes the sandwich better, then I'm willing to bet that adding bacon, greens, and tomatoes to an egg salad does the same thing. (Spoiler: It does.)

Prep time 15 minutes
Serves 6

12 Hard-Cooked Eggs (page 93)
2 tablespoons (28 g) Paleo-Friendly Mayonnaise (page 230)
2 tablespoons (28 ml) Paleo-Friendly Ranch Dressing (page 237)
2 tablespoons (30 g) Dijon mustard

1 tablespoon (15 ml) red wine vinegar
1 cup (30 g) torn baby spinach
1 cup (150 g) diced cherry or grape tomatoes
8 slices of cooked bacon, crumbled
¼ teaspoon sea salt

1 Peel and dice the eggs. Place them in a large bowl.

2 Add the Paleo-Friendly Mayonnaise, Paleo-Friendly Ranch Dressing, mustard, and vinegar. Smash everything together with a fork until creamy and well mixed.

3 Stir in the spinach, tomatoes, bacon, and salt. Taste and add more salt if needed.

4 Serve alone or spoon into lettuce cups.

Balsamic Poached Eggs with Prosciutto-Wrapped Asparagus

The nice thing about poaching eggs in a pressure cooker is that you can do multiple eggs at once! This simple yet elegant recipe would be perfect for a small group brunch.

Prep time 15 minutes
Pressure time 3-4 minutes + 10-15 minutes roasting time
Serves 4

2 teaspoons (10 ml) balsamic vinegar
4 eggs
Sea salt and black pepper

1 pound (455 g) asparagus
3 ounces (85 g) prosciutto
1 tablespoon (15 ml) avocado oil

1 Preheat the oven to 425°F (220°C, or gas mark 7).

2 Put 1 cup (235 ml) of water and the wire rack in the bottom of the pot.

3 Put ½ teaspoon of balsamic vinegar into each egg poaching cup. Crack an egg into each cup and sprinkle each egg with a generous pinch of salt and pepper. Carefully place the cups on top of the wire rack.

4 Close the lid and the steam valve. Set the cooker to high pressure for 3 or 4 minutes, depending on how runny you'd like your egg yolk.

5 Trim the asparagus and group them in bundles of four. (You should have four, maybe five bundles.) Wrap a piece or two of prosciutto around each bundle. Place the bundles on a small baking pan and drizzle the avocado oil over the top.

6 Roast the bundles for 10-15 minutes until the asparagus is tender and the prosciutto is crisp.

7 When the eggs are finished cooking, release the pressure manually. Remove the egg cups from the cooker and using a spoon, scoop the eggs out of the cups and on top of each asparagus bundle.

4

BEST BEEF

Of all of the types of shredded meat, I get most excited about shredded beef. I love the earthy flavor of beef and how well it complements bold, exciting flavors. The recipes in this chapter range from classic flavors of mushrooms and herbs to spicy Asian chili and everything in between.

Recipes

Green Chile Shredded Beef

This spunky, flavorful shredded beef should be a staple in your Tex-Mex recipe collection. My go-to is a giant salad with a little of this beef, lots of fresh vegetables, and some spicy ranch dressing. It also freezes well, so make extra to make your future self happy.

Prep time 15 minutes

Pressure time 70 minutes + 20–30 minutes natural release

Serves 8-10

One 3- to 4-pound (1.4–1.8 kg) beef roast

1 tablespoon (15 g) sea salt

2 teaspoons (4 g) ground cumin

½ teaspoon black pepper

2 tablespoons (28 ml) avocado oil or ghee (page 234)

One 15-ounce (425 g) jar salsa verde

1 large onion, diced (about 1½ cups [240 g])

1 tablespoon (10 g) minced garlic

1 medium poblano pepper, seeded (if desired) and diced

1 Cut the roast into 3 similar-size pieces. Sprinkle the salt, cumin, and pepper over the roast chunks and rub it in well.

2 Set the cooker to high sauté. Add the avocado oil to the pot. When the cooker has preheated, add the roast pieces to the pot. Sear them on a couple of sides until a nice golden crust has formed. Remove the meat from the pot and set aside.

3 Pour the salsa into the pot and stir it around to dislodge the crispy bits that may have stuck to the bottom. Add the onion, garlic, and chopped poblano pepper to the pot. Return the meat to the pot.

4 Close the lid and the steam valve. Set the cooker for 70 minutes on high pressure. Allow the cooker to release all of the pressure manually. It might take 20–30 minutes for this.

5 Remove the beef from the pot with a pair of tongs. Shred the beef and return the meat to the pot and mix with the salsa juices. Let the meat soak up some of the juices. If there is too much liquid for your liking, remove the meat with tongs and transfer to a serving dish.

6 Serve with a vegetable side dish or over a big taco salad with all the fixings.

Mediterranean Stuffed Collard Leaves

I think collards are sometimes an overlooked leafy green. Because of its sturdy texture, it can hold up to long cooking times and be used as a wrap for un-wiches and filled and baked into little packets. You'll love this flavorful Mediterranean version! It's also great as a weekend meal prep recipe to reheat for easy lunches during the week.

Prep time 30 minutes

Pressure time 18 minutes + 15 minutes natural release

Serves 6

8-10 collard leaves

1 pound (455 g) ground beef

⅓ cup (53 g) minced sweet onion

2 teaspoons minced garlic

1 teaspoon sea salt

1 teaspoon ground coriander

½ teaspoon dried oregano

½ teaspoon dried mint

¼ teaspoon dried dill

⅛ teaspoon cayenne pepper

1 egg

⅓ cup (37 g) almond flour

For the sauce:

One 15-ounce (425 g) can tomato sauce

3 tablespoons (45 ml) red wine vinegar

1 tablespoon (10 g) minced garlic

½ teaspoon ground coriander

¼ teaspoon sea salt

Pinch of cayenne pepper

1 tablespoon (8 g) tapioca or (9 g) arrowroot flour

¼ cup (60 ml) water

1 Prepare the cooker by putting ½ cup (120 ml) of water in the pot with the wire rack.

2 Wash and trim the stems from the collard leaves. Stack them in the cooker on the wire rack. Close the lid and the steam valve. Set the cooker to steam for 2 minutes. Prepare a bowl of ice water. When the collards are finished steaming, do a quick release of the pressure and dip them into the ice bath to stop the cooking. Lay them on a clean kitchen towel.

3 While the collards are steaming, start prepping the filling by putting the ground beef in a large bowl. Add the onion, garlic, spices, herbs, egg, and almond flour. Mix everything together gently with your hands until well combined. Divide the mixture into portions according to the number of collard leaves you have.

4 Start assembling the packets by placing a leaf on a flat surface with the stem end pointing away from you. Grab a portion of meat and form a small ball, somewhat flattened. Place it in the middle of the leaf. Fold the end closest to you over the meat and then fold the sides in. Roll the leaf away from you to form a packet. Repeat with each of the leaves and the portions of meat. Lay the packets on the wire rack and stack them if you need to.

5 To make the sauce, whisk together the sauce ingredients (except the tapioca flour and water) and pour it over the collard packets.

6 Close the lid and the steam valve. Set the cooker to high pressure for 18 minutes and then let the cooker release the pressure on its own for 15 minutes. Release any remaining pressure manually.

7 Transfer the collard packets to a serving dish and cover to keep warm. Remove the wire rack from the pot. Turn on the cooker to the high sauté setting. Whisk together the tapioca flour and water and stir it into the tomato sauce in the pot. Simmer for 2-3 minutes until the sauce has thickened.

8 Serve the collard packets with the sauce.

Gyro-Inspired Shredded Beef and Tzatziki Sauce

This tender shredded beef with Middle Eastern flavors goes perfectly with creamy tzatziki sauce. If you'd like your beef similar to gyro meat in texture, try crisping it up in the oven after you shred it. I included some notes in the recipe about it!

Prep time 15 minutes

Pressure time 1 hour +
15 minutes natural release

Serves 6-8

Note: If you'd prefer to have the meat a little crispy on the edges, put it on a rimmed baking sheet, drizzle with some of the cooking juices, and put it under the broiler for 10–12 minutes until some of the edges are golden brown and crisp, carnitas style.

2 tablespoons (28 ml) avocado oil

One 2- to 3-pound (900–1365 g) beef roast

4 teaspoons (5 g) Middle Eastern Seasoning (page 245), divided

2 teaspoons sea salt

1 red onion, halved and thinly sliced, divided

1 tablespoon (10 g) minced garlic

½ cup (120 ml) beef broth, homemade (page 242) or store-bought, or water

Pinch of crushed red pepper flakes

1 tablespoon (15 ml) freshly squeezed lemon juice

For the paleo tzatziki:

½ cup (115 g) Paleo-Friendly Mayonnaise (page 230)

¼ cup (60 ml) coconut milk

½ cup (68 g) grated cucumber

1 teaspoon minced garlic

¼ teaspoon sea salt

1 heaping tablespoon (4 g) chopped fresh dill or flat-leaf parsley

1 tablespoon (15 ml) freshly squeezed lemon juice

1 Turn the cooker to the high sauté setting and add the avocado oil to the pot.

2 Cut the beef in half and sprinkle the pieces with 3 teaspoons (4 g) of the Middle Eastern Seasoning and the salt. Put the pieces in the pot and sear on two sides, 3-4 minutes each, to form a golden crust. Turn the cooker off.

3 Reserve a few slices of onion to mince and save for the tzatziki. (You should have about 1 tablespoon [10 g] of minced onion.) Put the rest of the onion, garlic, and beef broth in the pot and sprinkle with red pepper flakes.

4 Close the lid and the steam valve. Set the cooker to high pressure for 60 minutes. Let the cooker release pressure naturally for 15 minutes and then release any remaining pressure manually.

5 Meanwhile, make the tzatziki. Combine the Paleo-Friendly Mayonnaise, coconut milk, grated cucumber, garlic, salt, dill, lemon juice, and the reserved minced onion. Chill for at least 20-30 minutes for best flavor.

6 Remove the beef from the cooker, shred it with two forks, and then return it to the pot. Drizzle the lemon juice over the beef.

7 Serve the shredded beef over a bed of Roasted Cauliflower Rice (page 200) or salad greens with a drizzle of the tzatziki.

Pot Roast with Balsamic Gravy

If you've never had balsamic gravy, you're missing out, my friends. It's dark, rich, and tangy and adds a fun twist on a traditional pot roast.

Prep time 15 minutes

Pressure time 60 minutes + 15–20 minutes natural release

Serves 8-10

2 tablespoons (28 ml) avocado oil

One 2- to 3-pound (900–1365 g) beef roast

2 teaspoons sea salt

1 cup (160 g) diced sweet onion

½ cup (120 ml) balsamic vinegar

1 tablespoon (10 g) minced garlic

1 tablespoon (16 g) tomato paste

1 teaspoon coarsely ground black pepper (or cracked peppercorns)

Pinch of crushed red pepper flakes

3 sprigs of fresh rosemary or ¼ teaspoon dried crushed rosemary

⅔ cup (160 ml) beef broth, homemade (page 242) or store-bought

1 tablespoon (8 g) tapioca or (9 g) arrowroot flour

1 Turn the cooker to the high sauté setting and add the avocado oil to the pot.

2 Cut the roast into 2 or 3 large pieces. Sprinkle the salt over the meat. Put the roast pieces into the pot and sear on two sides, 3–4 minutes each. Turn the cooker off.

3 Add the onion to the pot. Whisk together the vinegar, garlic, and tomato paste and then pour it over the beef. Sprinkle the black pepper and red pepper flakes on the meat and lay the rosemary on top.

4 Close the lid and the steam valve. Set the cooker to high pressure for 60 minutes. Let all of the pressure release naturally—this should take 15–20 minutes.

5 Transfer the beef to a large plate and break it up into large 2- to 3-inch (5 to 7.5 cm) pieces.

6 Turn the cooker to high sauté. Whisk together the beef broth and tapioca flour and while whisking the pot juices, slowly add the broth slurry. Cook for 2–3 minutes until the juices become bubbly and slightly thickened into a gravy.

7 Serve the beef with the gravy. (Mashed potatoes are highly recommended here.)

Ultimate Mushroom Pot Roast

If you've never pulverized dried mushrooms, I think you should do it soon. It's such an easy to way to add richness and more umami flavor to beef. And if you happen to love mushrooms, it's another way to incorporate more mushroom flavor!

Prep time 20 minutes
Pressure time 90 minutes +
15 minutes natural release
Serves 8

One 3- to 4-pound (1.4–1.8 kg) beef roast
½ ounce (15 g) dried mixed mushrooms
2 teaspoons (2 g) dried thyme
1 tablespoon (15 g) sea salt
Pinch of crushed red pepper flakes
2 tablespoons (28 ml) avocado oil
1 medium sweet onion, chopped
2 large carrots, peeled and cut into ½-inch (1.3 cm) pieces

2 celery stalks, diced
10 ounces (280 g) sliced cremini or baby bella mushrooms
½ cup (120 ml) beef broth, homemade (page 242) or store-bought, or water
¼ cup (60 ml) coconut aminos
1 tablespoon (16 g) tomato paste
1 tablespoon (15 ml) red wine vinegar

1 Cut the roast in into 2 or 3 pieces if you have one closer to 4 pounds (1.8 kg). Place it on a rimmed baking sheet.

2 Pulverize the dried mushrooms in a food processor or blender. You could also put them in a plastic zip-top bag and crush them with a rolling pin. Combine the pulverized mushrooms with the thyme, salt, and red pepper flakes in a small bowl. Rub the mixture all over the pieces of roast.

3 Put the avocado oil in the pressure cooker and set it to high sauté. When the pot has preheated, place the roast pieces inside (you may need to do this in two batches). Sear on two sides, 3–4 minutes per side. Turn the cooker off. Transfer the beef back to the baking sheet.

4 Add the onion, carrots, celery, and mushrooms to the pot. Whisk together the beef broth, coconut aminos, and tomato paste. Pour it into the pot. Return the beef to the pot and nestle it among the vegetables.

5 Close the lid and the steam valve. Set the cooker to high pressure for 90 minutes. Let the cooker release pressure naturally for 15 minutes and then release any remaining pressure manually.

6 At this point, you can serve the roast with the vegetables and cooking juices or you can blend the juices and vegetables into a smooth gravy using an immersion blender or a countertop blender. Taste the gravy and add the red wine vinegar and a pinch or two of salt, if needed.

7 Serve the roast with the gravy and your desired side dish.

Veggie-Packed Taco Meat

When my kids were younger, I used to hide minced vegetables in their taco meat and anything else that would mask them—like Sloppy Joes, chili, and curries. They ate them right up and never knew the difference! This pressure cooker taco meat has a different texture than traditional taco meat. The vegetables add more moisture and the overall texture is softer and more like a Bolognese sauce, which makes it perfect for rice bowls or on big taco salads.

Prep time: 20 minutes
Pressure time: 10 minutes + 10 minutes natural release
Serves 8-10

1 pound (455 g) ground beef

4 tablespoons (30 g) taco seasoning

2 tablespoons (10 g) dried minced onion or 2 teaspoons onion powder

Two 4-ounce (115 g) cans diced green chiles

1 medium zucchini

8 ounces (225 g) sliced mushrooms

1 bell pepper

1 cup (120 g) riced cauliflower

One 8-ounce (225 g) can tomato sauce

1 cup (235 ml) water

1 lime

½ cup (8 g) chopped fresh cilantro

Roasted Cauliflower Rice (page 200), jasmine rice, Steamed Whole Potatoes (page 183), or salad greens, for serving

Chopped avocado, for garnish

Hot sauce, for serving

1 Turn the cooker to the high sauté setting and add the ground beef. Cook the beef, stirring often and breaking the meat into small bits, until it starts to form a golden crust, about 15 minutes. Add the taco seasoning, dried minced onion, and diced green chiles, stir, and then turn off the cooker.

2 Meanwhile, prep the zucchini, mushrooms, and bell pepper. You can mince them (I recommend using a food processor) or chop them into a small dice, whatever your preference is. I find my kids liked it better when it was minced because it blended into the texture of the meat better.

3 Add the minced vegetables to the pot along with the riced cauliflower, tomato sauce, and water. Give it a stir and then close the pot and the steam valve.

4 Set the cooker to high pressure for 10 minutes. Let the cooker release the pressure naturally for 10 minutes, and then manually release the rest.

5 Open the lid and stir. If the mixture is too watery, turn to the sauté setting to cook off some of the liquid. The meat-veggie mixture will be soft and the consistency of a thick chili. Stir in the juice from ½ of the lime and the cilantro. Taste and add more lime juice, salt, or cilantro, if necessary.

6 This recipe is best suited for bowl or salad-type meals (as opposed to spooning it into a tortilla because it can get very messy). Serve over cauliflower or jasmine rice, in a steamed potato, or on a bed of salad greens and top with chopped avocado, hot sauce, and any other of your favorite taco toppings.

Classic Bolognese

After doing some research on authentic Bolognese, I found out that none of them contained herbs! That was surprising to me, but I'm sure adding some fresh basil to this sauce wouldn't take it in a bad direction.

Prep time 30 minutes

Pressure time 5 minutes + 10 minutes natural release

Serves 8

1 tablespoon (15 ml) ghee (page 234) or (14 g) grass-fed butter

1 tablespoon (15 ml) avocado oil

½ cup (80 g) diced sweet onion

½ cup (60 g) diced celery

½ cup (65 g) diced carrot

1 teaspoon minced garlic

4 ounces (115 g) uncooked bacon or pancetta, diced

1 pound (455 g) ground pork

1 pound (455 g) ground beef

2 tablespoons (32 g) tomato paste

1 cup (235 ml) unsweetened almond milk

1 cup (235 ml) beef broth, homemade (page 242) or store-bought

One 28-ounce (785 g) can crushed tomatoes (San Marzano, if possible)

2 teaspoons sea salt

½ teaspoon black pepper

2 tablespoons (28 ml) red wine vinegar

1 Turn the cooker to high sauté and add the ghee and avocado oil to the pot. When it has preheated, add the onion, celery, carrot, and garlic. Sauté for a few minutes until the onion has become soft and translucent.

2 Add the bacon and cook, stirring often, until the meat is cooked through and somewhat crisp.

3 Add the ground pork and beef in three batches, stirring, and breaking up the meat as it cooks. Let each addition cook mostly through before adding the next one. There should be some meat drippings in the bottom of pot, but if it looks too soupy or greasy, drain off some of it.

4 Stir in the tomato paste and then add the milk, beef broth, tomatoes, salt, pepper, and vinegar.

5 Close the lid and the steam valve. Set the cooker to high pressure for 5 minutes. Let the cooker release the pressure on its own for 10 minutes or so before releasing the rest of the pressure.

6 Taste and add more salt or vinegar if necessary. Serve over squash noodles or your choice of side dish.

Notes:

• *This Bolognese is actually better the next day and thickens up quite a bit after being chilled and reheated.*

• *I wouldn't suggest using coconut milk as a replacement for the almond milk.*

BBQ Bacon Meatloaf and Potatoes

I feel like a superhero when I can make an entire meal in one pot. This meatloaf cooks over creamy potatoes and everything is coated in a tangy, simple BBQ sauce. There's a bit of prep time involved in this one, but only having to wash one pot makes it worth it.

Prep time 40 minutes

Pressure time 20 minutes + 10 minutes natural release

Serves 6

10 ounces (280 g) uncooked bacon, cut into 1-inch (2.5 cm) pieces

1 pound (455 g) ground beef

1 pound (455 g) ground pork

3 tablespoons (45 ml) coconut aminos

1 tablespoon (5 g) dried minced onion

1 tablespoon (10 g) minced garlic

1 teaspoon sea salt

1 egg

⅓ cup (37 g) blanched almond flour

½ cup (120 ml) beef broth, homemade (page 242) or store-bought

Two 15-ounce (425 g) cans tomato sauce

½ cup (120 ml) apple cider vinegar

⅓ cup (115 g) honey

1½ teaspoons onion powder

3 pounds (1.4 kg) red or Yukon gold potatoes

1 Turn the cooker to the medium sauté setting and place the bacon in the pot. Cook the bacon until it is crispy, stirring often. This will probably take about 20 minutes.

2 Meanwhile, combine the ground beef, pork, coconut aminos, dried minced onion, garlic, salt, egg, and almond flour in a large bowl. Use your hands to gently mix everything together—avoid squeezing it in your fists.

3 When the bacon is finished cooking, transfer it to the meatloaf bowl and combine it with the meat mixture. Set aside.

4 Remove all but 1–2 tablespoons (15–28 ml) of bacon drippings from the pot. Add the beef broth to the pot and scrape the bits off the bottom of the pot. Turn off the cooker.

5 Combine the tomato sauce, vinegar, honey, and onion powder in a bowl.

6 If your potatoes are larger than 3 inches (7.5 cm) long or 2 inches (5 cm) wide, cut them in half. Arrange them on the bottom of the pot. Pour 1 cup (235 ml) of the tomato sauce mixture over the potatoes and place the rack on top of the potatoes, making it as flat and even as you can.

7 Tear off two sheets of aluminum foil about 18 inches (45 cm) long each. Fold each in half lengthwise, then in half again lengthwise to form a long strip. Place each strip into the cooker on the wire rack, forming an x-shaped "sling."

8 Form the meatloaf mixture into a thick, round pancake shape. It should not be more than 2 inches (5 cm) thick. Place the meat on top of the foil sling on top of the X. Pour 1 cup (235 ml) of the tomato sauce mixture over the meatloaf.

9 Close the lid and the steam valve. Set the cooker to high pressure for 20 minutes. Let the cooker release pressure on its own for 10 minutes and then release the rest of the pressure manually.

10 Transfer the meatloaf and potatoes to a large serving platter. Cover to keep warm.

11 Pour the remaining tomato sauce mixture into the pot and turn the cooker to the high sauté setting. Simmer the BBQ sauce for about 5 minutes until heated through.

12 Slice the meatloaf and serve it with the potatoes and BBQ sauce.

Sambal Short Ribs with Mushrooms

Sambal oelek is one of my favorite ingredients for adding heat to Asian-style recipes. It adds not only a punch of heat but also garlic flavor. You can also use Asian chili garlic paste or sriracha if you have trouble finding sambal oelek.

Prep time 20 minutes
Pressure time 50 minutes + 15 minutes natural release
Serves 4

2 tablespoons (28 ml) avocado oil

1 tablespoon (15 ml) sesame oil

1 teaspoon sea salt, divided

½ teaspoon black pepper

4 pounds (1.8 kg) meaty bone-in beef short ribs

1 cup (160 g) chopped sweet onion

3 large portobello mushrooms, sliced

1 cup (235 ml) beef broth, homemade (page 242) or store-bought

3 tablespoons (45 ml) coconut aminos

2 tablespoons (30 g) sambal oelek or Asian chili garlic paste

1 tablespoon (10 g) minced garlic

1 tablespoon (8 g) finely grated ginger

4 scallions, thinly sliced

1 Set the cooker to high sauté. Put the avocado oil and sesame oil into the pot.

2 Sprinkle ½ teaspoon of the salt and the pepper over both sides of the ribs. When the cooker has preheated, sear the short ribs (in batches, if they don't all fit) for 3-4 minutes on each side to form golden brown crusts. Transfer the ribs to a large plate.

3 Add the onion to the pot and cook for 3-4 minutes until the onion has softened. Add the mushrooms and cook for another 3-4 minutes.

4 Add the rest of the ingredients (except the scallions) as well as the remaining ½ teaspoon of salt to the pot. Stir well. Turn off the sauté mode.

5 Add the ribs back to the pot. Close the lid and the steam valve. Set the cooker to high pressure for 50 minutes. Let the cooker release all of the pressure naturally.

6 Serve the short ribs with a couple of spoonfuls of the mushrooms and sauce with your desired side dish.

Recommended side dish: Roasted Cauliflower Rice (page 200)

Tex-Mex Meatloaf with Nacho Cheeze Sauce

This is a fun Tex-Mex take on meatloaf with a touch of heat. I especially love drizzling the Spicy Nacho Sauce on it during serving. You could also add some baked sweet potato chips to this and turn it into a nacho-like meal!

Prep time 15 minutes

Pressure time 18 minutes + 5 minutes natural release

Serves 6

1½ pounds (680 g) ground beef

One 4-ounce (115 g) can diced green chiles

3 tablespoons (23 g) taco seasoning

1 tablespoon (15 ml) hot sauce

1 egg

⅓ cup (37 g) almond flour

½ recipe Spicy Nacho Sauce (page 240)

1 Combine the ground beef, green chiles, taco seasoning, hot sauce, egg, and almond flour in a large bowl. Use your hands to gently mix everything well and form the mixture into a 2-inch (5 cm)-thick round "loaf."

2 Prepare the cooker by putting 1 cup (235 ml) of water and the wire rack on the bottom. Tear off two sheets of aluminum foil about 18 inches (45 cm) long. Fold each in half lengthwise, then in half again length-wise to form a long strip. Place each strip into the cooker on the wire rack, forming an x-shaped "sling."

3 Place the meatloaf on the foil sling inside the pot.

4 Close the lid and the steam valve. Set the cooker to high pressure for 18 minutes. Let the cooker release pressure naturally for 5 minutes before releasing the rest of the pressure manually.

5 Meanwhile, make the Spicy Nacho Sauce, if you haven't already. If you need to warm it up, put it into a small saucepan and heat it over medium-low heat, whisking often.

6 Lift the meatloaf out of the pot and transfer it to a serving dish. Pour half of the Spicy Nacho Sauce over the meatloaf. Slice and serve with more sauce.

Classic Garlic Herb Short Ribs and Gravy

One of my favorite ways to thicken gravy is to add some aromatics to the pan and blend all of the pan sauces and vegetables after the meat has cooked. You end up with a creamy, hearty gravy without any thickeners!

Prep time 30 minutes

Pressure time 55 minutes + 15 minutes natural release

Serves 6

4 pounds (1.8 kg) beef short ribs, cut into 1- or 2-rib portions

2 teaspoons sea salt

½ teaspoon black pepper

4 tablespoons (60 ml) avocado oil

½ cup (80 g) diced sweet onion

½ cup (65 g) diced carrot

½ cup (60 g) diced celery

1 tablespoon (10 g) minced garlic

¼ teaspoon whole black peppercorns

Pinch of crushed red pepper flakes

½ cup (120 ml) red wine or unsweetened grape or pomegranate juice

1 cup (235 ml) beef broth, homemade (page 242) or store-bought

3–4 large sprigs of fresh thyme or 1 teaspoon dried thyme

3–4 large sprigs of fresh rosemary or 2 teaspoons dried rosemary

½ lemon (optional)

1 Put the short ribs on a sheet pan. Sprinkle them with the salt and pepper.

2 Set the cooker to high sauté. When it has preheated, add half of the short ribs. Sear on two sides (any two sides) for 3–4 minutes each side. Transfer the ribs back to the sheet pan. Repeat with the remaining short ribs.

3 Add the onion, carrot, and celery to the pot. Sauté for 2–3 minutes until the vegetables soften slightly. Add the garlic, peppercorns, and red pepper flakes. Add the wine to deglaze any bits stuck to the bottom of the pot. Stir in the beef broth.

4 Return the ribs to the pot, nestling them in with the vegetables. You'll have to layer them on top of each other. Put the fresh thyme and rosemary on top of the beef.

5 Close the lid and the steam valve. Set the cooker to high pressure for 55 minutes. Let the cooker release pressure naturally for 15 minutes before releasing the rest of the pressure manually.

6 Remove the short ribs from the pot. Skim off some of the oil from the top if you like. Blend the pot juices together to form a smooth gravy. Taste it and add a squeeze of lemon juice and a pinch or two of salt if you feel it needs it.

7 Return the short ribs to the pot to soak up some of the juices. Serve the ribs and gravy with your desired side dish.

Home-Brined Corned Beef and Cabbage

I'm ashamed to admit that I was far into adulthood before I realized that corned beef had nothing to do with corn. And that I had been missing out on a tasty brined beef roast for longer than I should have. I'm making up for lost time with this easy recipe. Just save some leftovers to make a hash later in the week!

Prep time 15 minutes + cooling and brining time

Pressure time 90 minutes + 10 minutes natural release

Serves 8

Note: If you like, you can substitute part of the broth with a bottle of dark Guinness beer for a more traditional Irish flavor.

1 cup (240 g) kosher salt

½ cup (72 g) coconut sugar

¼ cup (25 g) pickling spices, divided

12 whole juniper berries, divided

2 cinnamon sticks, divided

2 pounds (900 g) ice cubes (about 6 cups)

One 3- to 4-pound (1.4–1.8 kg) beef brisket

½ large onion, cut into wedges

4 cloves of garlic, smashed

1 quart (946 ml) beef broth, homemade (page 242) or store-bought

4 large carrots, cut into ½-inch (1.3 cm) pieces

1 small head of cabbage, cut into wedges or large pieces

2 pounds (900 g) baby potatoes (1½–2 inches [3.8–5 cm] wide) or other white potatoes cut the same size

Whole-grain mustard, for serving (optional)

1 Put 2 quarts (1.9 L) of water in a large pot over high heat. Add the salt, coconut sugar, half of the pickling spices, half of the juniper berries, and 1 cinnamon stick to the pot. (Reserve the remaining spices for when you're ready to cook the brisket.)

2 Let the brine simmer until the sugar is dissolved and then remove it from the heat. Add the ice to the pot to cool the brine quickly. Refrigerate the brine until it is at least 45°F (7°C) or colder. This might take a few hours.

3 When the brine is ready, cut the brisket in half and put it and the cooled brine in a very large pot or container that will be used to hold the submerged brisket (and fit in your fridge) for several days. I found my 6-quart (5.7 L) pressure cooker insert pot worked well for this. Chill for at least 5 days and up to 10 days. If you have a hard time completely submerging the brisket, turn it once a day, so it brines evenly. If it floats to the top, put a sealed aluminum can (like a can of tomatoes) or a glass jar on top of it.

4 When you're ready to cook the brisket, prepare your pressure cooker by putting the rack in the bottom. Pull the brisket pieces out of the brine, rinse them off, and put them on the wire rack, laying flat. It's okay to stack them. Add the onion wedges and garlic on top of the beef and pour the beef broth over everything. Add the remaining pickling spices, juniper berries, and cinnamon stick.

5 Close the lid and the steam valve and set the cooker to high pressure for 90 minutes. Let the cooker release pressure naturally for 10 minutes before releasing the rest of the pressure manually. Transfer the beef to a serving plate and cover to keep it warm.

6 Use a slotted spoon or a spider skimmer to remove the onion, garlic, and large spices from the pot. Add the carrots, cabbage, and potatoes to the pot. Close the lid and the steam valve and set the cooker to high pressure for 4 minutes. Do a quick release when the vegetables are finished cooking.

7 Transfer the vegetables to the platter with the corned beef, discarding the cooking liquid.

8 Serve with whole grain mustard, if you like.

Cracked Pepper Tri-Tip with Bacon-Onion Jam

Tri-tip is a fabulous cut of beef, but in all honesty, the star of this show is the Bacon-Onion Jam. It complements the peppery beef so well and has lots of other uses, too! It's great on meatloaf, grilled meats and vegetables and stirred into soup.

Prep time 40 minutes

Pressure time 45 minutes + 15 minutes natural release

Serves 8

For the Bacon-Onion Jam:

1 pound (455 g) uncooked bacon, diced

3 large sweet onions, thinly sliced

¼ cup (60 ml) apple cider vinegar

⅔ cup (160 ml) chicken or beef broth, homemade (page 242) or store-bought

2 tablespoons (18 g) coconut sugar

Pinch of dried thyme

Pinch of kosher salt

For the tri-tips:

One 2- to 3-pound (900–1365 g) tri-tip roast

1 tablespoon (10 g) whole peppercorns

1 tablespoon (15 g) kosher salt

1 teaspoon coarsely ground black pepper

1 cup (160 g) diced sweet onion

¼ cup (60 ml) beef broth, homemade (page 242) or store-bought

2 tablespoons (28 ml) coconut aminos

2 teaspoons minced garlic

3 sprigs of fresh rosemary

1 To make the Bacon-Onion Jam, put the bacon in a large skillet over medium heat and cook, stirring often, until crispy, 15–20 minutes. Transfer the bacon to a paper towel–lined plate for later. Put 2–3 tablespoons (28–45 ml) of the bacon drippings in the pressure cooker pot. Leave the rest in the skillet.

2 Return the skillet to medium-high heat and add the onions. Cook, stirring occasionally, until they have softened and have begun to turn slightly golden brown. Cover, turn the heat to medium-low, and let the onions cook and caramelize for another 20 minutes or so, stirring occasionally, until they're deeply browned. If they start getting too dark too quickly, reduce the heat.

3 Meanwhile, place the tri-tip on a large plate. Put the peppercorns in a small zip-top baggie and whack it with a rolling pin a few dozen times to crack them up. Rub them, the kosher salt, and the coarsely ground pepper all over the tri-tip. Cut the roast in half.

4 Turn the cooker to the high sauté setting. Sear the pieces of tri-tip, one at a time, letting them cook undisturbed on each side for 3–4 minutes.

5 Set the roast pieces back on the plate and add the 1 cup (160 g) of diced onion to the pot. Cook for a few minutes until the onion softens. Add the ¼ cup (60 ml) of beef broth and scrape up any bits from the bottom of the pot. Add the coconut aminos, garlic, and rosemary and then add the seared beef back to the pot.

Note: The tri-tip cut was popularized in California and has gradually made its way into other parts of the United States. If you have trouble finding this cut, you can ask your butcher for a triangle steak or a bottom sirloin steak.

6 Cover the pot and close the steam valve. Set it to high pressure for 45 minutes. Let the pressure go down naturally—or at least 15 minutes before releasing it manually.

7 When the caramelized onions in your skillet are nice and deep golden brown, add the bacon to the skillet as well as the vinegar, ⅔ cup (160 ml) of beef broth, coconut sugar, thyme, and salt.

8 Increase the heat to medium-high and cook until the liquid has reduced by half. Remove the skillet from the heat and let it cool for a few minutes. Transfer the bacon-onion mixture to a food processor or a blender. Pulse until the larger chunks have broken down and the mixture is more jamlike.

9 When the tri-tip is finished cooking, slice the roast and return the pieces to the pot juices.

10 Serve the tri-tip with a drizzle of cooking juices and a spoonful of the Bacon-Onion Jam.

Ancho Flank Steak with Shishito Cabbage Slaw

Shishito peppers have become popular recently and are a great option if you're looking for a mild chile pepper. They raise this simple cabbage slaw to a whole other level! If you can't find shishitos, Anaheim peppers are a good, mild substitution. Poblano peppers or jalapeño peppers are good if you want to add more heat to the slaw.

Prep time 25 minutes

Pressure time 15 minutes + 5 minutes natural release

Serves 6

Note: You can serve the beef and slaw in lettuce wraps or paleo-friendly tortillas, too.

2 pounds (900 g) flank steak, sliced against the grain into ¼-inch (6 mm)-thick pieces

2 teaspoons ancho chile powder

1½ teaspoons onion powder

1 teaspoon sea salt

1 teaspoon smoked paprika

¼ teaspoon cayenne pepper

1 tablespoon (16 g) tomato paste

½ cup (120 ml) beef broth, homemade (page 242) or store-bought

For the slaw:

1 tablespoon (15 ml) avocado oil

6 ounces (170 g) shishito peppers

½ large head of green or purple cabbage, thinly sliced or shredded

3 scallions, thinly sliced

Juice from ½ lime

1 tablespoon (15 ml) extra-virgin olive oil

½ teaspoon minced garlic

½ cup (8 g) chopped fresh cilantro or parsley

Generous pinch of sea salt

Hot sauce, for serving

Sliced avocado, for serving

1 Put the flank steak in a bowl or on a rimmed baking sheet—some container you can mix the beef in.

2 Sprinkle the chile powder, onion powder, salt, paprika, and cayenne pepper on the beef. Use your hands to spread the seasonings around and coat the meat thoroughly.

3 Put the tomato paste and the beef broth in the pressure cooker pot and whisk them together. Add the beef to the pot.

4 Close the lid and the steam valve. Set the cooker to high pressure for 15 minutes. Let the cooker release pressure naturally for 5 minutes before releasing the pressure manually.

5 To make the slaw, while the beef is cooking, put the avocado oil in a large skillet over medium-high heat. Add the peppers to the skillet and cook, flipping them around every couple of minutes, until most of the peppers are covered with dark, blistered spots and are soft.

6 Transfer the peppers to a cutting board and let them cool for a few minutes until you can handle them with your bare hands.

7 Meanwhile, combine the cabbage, scallions, lime juice, olive oil, garlic, cilantro, and salt in a large bowl.

8 Cut the tops from the shishito peppers and cut a slit into them with a knife. Scrape the large clump of seeds out and slice the rest of the pepper into strips. Add the sliced peppers to the bowl with the cabbage and toss to combine.

9 Serve the beef with a drizzle of pan juices, a side of slaw, and some hot sauce and avocado slices.

Mongolian Beef

My husband and I loved the Mongolian beef at a popular upscale Chinese restaurant chain. I wanted to create my own version that wasn't quite as syrupy sweet, but still had all of the deep, Asian flavors that we love.

Prep time 15 minutes

Pressure time 12 minutes + 5 minutes natural release

Serves 6

2 pounds (900 g) flank steak, halved and thinly sliced against the grain (¼–½ inch [6–13 mm] wide)

1 teaspoon sea salt

1 teaspoon onion powder

⅔ cup (160 ml) coconut aminos

2 tablespoons (28 ml) fish sauce

3-inch (7.5 cm) knob ginger, finely grated

2 teaspoons minced garlic

¼ cup (60 ml) rice vinegar

Pinch of crushed red pepper flakes

½ cup (120 ml) water, divided

2 tablespoons (16 g) tapioca flour

2–3 tablespoons (40–60 g) honey, to taste

1 small bunch of scallions, trimmed and cut into 1½- to 2-inch (3.8–5 cm) pieces

Roasted Cauliflower Rice (page 200) or steamed jasmine rice, for serving

1 Put the flank steak in the pot of your pressure cooker. Sprinkle with the salt and onion powder and toss it with your hands or a pair of tongs to spread the seasonings evenly.

2 In a large glass measuring cup or a bowl, whisk together the coconut aminos, fish sauce, ginger, garlic, vinegar, red pepper flakes, and ¼ cup (60 ml) of the water. Pour it over the beef.

3 Close the lid and the steam valve and set the cooker to high pressure for 12 minutes. Let the pressure release naturally for 5 minutes before releasing the rest of the pressure manually.

4 Use a slotted spoon or a spider skimmer to remove the beef pieces from the pot and set them on a plate. Whisk together the remaining ¼ cup (60 ml) of water with the tapioca flour. Set the cooker to high sauté and whisk in the tapioca slurry. Continue to whisk the sauce until it thickens, about 2 minutes. Turn off the cooker and whisk in the honey. Return the beef to the pot and stir to coat it in the sauce. Stir in the scallions.

5 Serve over cauliflower rice or steamed jasmine rice.

Chinese BBQ Beef Stew

I have always loved hoisin sauce, but when I started paying attention to ingredient labels, I was shocked at how much sugar it contained. The sauce that is poured over the meat and vegetables in step 4 is a great homemade hoisin sauce that also works well in stir-fries.

Prep time 30 minutes

Pressure time 20 minutes + 10 minutes natural release

Serves 6

1½ pounds (680 g) beef stew meat, cut into 1-inch (2.5 cm) pieces if needed

1½ teaspoons sea salt

½ teaspoon black pepper

2 tablespoons (12 g) minced or (16 g) finely grated ginger, divided

2 tablespoons (28 ml) avocado oil, divided

1½ cups (240 g) diced sweet onion

1 cup (120 g) diced celery

3 large carrots, peeled and cut into ½-inch (1.3 cm) pieces

1½ pounds (680 g) turnips (about 3 large), peeled and cut into 1-inch (2.5 cm) pieces

½ cup (120 ml) coconut aminos

3 tablespoons (45 ml) fish sauce

3 tablespoons (48 g) almond butter or another type of nut butter

⅓ cup (80 ml) rice vinegar

3 tablespoons (60 g) molasses

1½ tablespoons (23 ml) sesame oil

1 tablespoon (6 g) minced garlic

1-3 teaspoons (5-15 g) Asian chili paste or sambal oelek

2 tablespoons (32 g) tomato paste

¼ cup (60 ml) water

1 tablespoon (8 g) tapioca flour

Handful of snow peas

Roasted Cauliflower Rice (page 200) or jasmine rice, for serving (optional)

Mung bean sprouts, for garnish

Chopped fresh cilantro, for garnish

Lime wedges, for garnish

1 Put the beef in a large bowl. Sprinkle with the salt, pepper, and 1 tablespoon (6 or 8 g) of the ginger.

2 Put 1 tablespoon (15 ml) of the avocado oil in the pressure cooker pot and set it on high sauté. When the pot has preheated, sear half of the beef for 3-4 minutes, flipping once or twice. Remove the beef from the pot, add the remaining 1 tablespoon (15 ml) of avocado oil, and then sear the other half of the beef. Remove the beef from the pot.

3 Add the onion, celery, and carrots to the pot. Sauté for 2-3 minutes until the vegetables have softened slightly. Turn off the cooker. Add the turnips to the pot.

4 Whisk together the coconut aminos, fish sauce, almond butter, vinegar, molasses, sesame oil, garlic, chili paste, tomato paste, and remaining 1 tablespoon (6 or 8 g) of ginger. Pour it over the meat and vegetables.

5 Close the lid and the steam valve. Set the cooker to high pressure for 20 minutes. Let the cooker release pressure naturally for 10 minutes before releasing the rest of the pressure manually.

6 Whisk together the water and tapioca flour. Stir the mixture into the stew as soon as you take the lid off. You shouldn't have to turn on the sauté mode in order for it to thicken. Add the snow peas and put the lid back on. Let them steam for 5 minutes or so to soften. (Don't pressurize.)

7 Serve the stew over a bed of rice (if desired) with a sprinkle of mung bean sprouts and a pinch or two of fresh cilantro, with the lime wedges on the side.

5

COMFORTING CHICKEN AND TURKEY

I've always wondered why chicken is so universally adored. Is it its versatility? Its mild, neutral flavor and lightness? Whatever the reason, there are sure to be recipes in this chapter using all cuts of chicken to please whatever palate you're cooking for.

Recipes

Garlic Roast Chicken and Gravy

The classic flavors in this roast chicken recipe are boosted by a few extra cloves of garlic. And by a few I mean eighteen. I hope that doesn't scare you off—garlic gets deliciously mild and creamy when cooked for a long time and you'll want to drink this gravy with a straw.

Prep time 20 minutes

Pressure time 25 minutes + 15 minutes natural release

Serves 6

1 cup (235 ml) chicken broth, homemade (page 242) or store-bought

½ large onion, cut into wedges

1 medium carrot, cut into 4-5 pieces

1 celery stalk, cut into 4-5 pieces

18 cloves of garlic, smashed

1 tablespoon (15 g) sea salt

1½ tablespoons (3 g) chopped fresh rosemary

1 teaspoon black pepper

One 3- to 4-pound (1.4-1.8 kg) whole chicken

3 tablespoons (45 ml) ghee (page 234) or avocado oil

1 tablespoon (8 g) tapioca starch (optional)

1 Put the chicken broth, onion, carrot, and celery in the pressure cooker pot. Put 6 of the smashed garlic cloves in the pot and place the wire rack on top, arranging the vegetables so the rack lies flat.

2 Combine the salt, rosemary, and pepper in a small bowl.

3 Use your fingers to loosen the skin from the flesh of the chicken around the breast areas. Cut a small ½-inch (1.3 cm) slit between the thigh and drumstick (so you can access both areas) and loosen the skin. Rub as much of the salt mixture under the skin and on the skin as you can— all over the chicken. Insert the remaining 12 cloves of smashed garlic under the skin, too.

4 Tie the legs together with kitchen twine and set the bird, breast-side up, on the wire rack. Drizzle with the ghee.

5 Close the lid and the steam valve and set the cooker to high pressure for 25 minutes. Let the cooker release pressure naturally for 15 minutes and then release any remaining pressure manually.

6 Transfer the chicken to a serving platter to rest and cover it to keep warm. Remove the wire rack and blend the contents of the pot with an immersion blender or a counter-top blender.

7 If you'd like the gravy to be a little thicker, remove 1 cup (235 ml) of it, whisk in the tapioca starch, and then slowly pour it back into the pot while whisking the rest of the gravy. Turn the cooker to the high sauté setting and simmer for a minute or two until it has thickened.

8 Carve the chicken and serve with the gravy.

Easy Faux-tisserie Chicken

It's nearly impossible to find a clean store-bought rotisserie chicken these days. Luckily, it's easy to make your own at home with very little effort. Feel free to play with the seasonings in this recipe and adjust them to your liking! Adding some classic herbs like dried thyme and rosemary to the rub would take it in a great direction, too.

Prep time 10 minutes + resting time for chicken

Pressure time 25 minutes + 15 minutes natural release

Serves 6

One 3- to 4-pound (1.4–1.8 kg) whole chicken
1 tablespoon (15 g) sea salt
1 teaspoon paprika
1 teaspoon onion powder

1 teaspoon granulated garlic
1 teaspoon dried thyme
¼ teaspoon black pepper
1 lemon

1 Place the chicken on a large plate and use a paper towel to pat the chicken dry. Rub the salt all over the chicken and then let it sit at room temperature for 20–30 minutes to take some of the chill off.

2 Combine the other seasonings with the juice from ½ of the lemon in a small bowl and then rub the mixture over the chicken as well, getting some under the skin if you can. Tie the legs together using kitchen twine.

3 Place the wire rack inside the cooker insert. Add 1 cup (235 ml) of water.

4 Place the chicken on top of the wire rack, breast-side up.

5 Close the lid and the steam valve. Set the cooker to high pressure for 25 minutes. Let the cooker release pressure naturally for 15 minutes and then release any remaining pressure manually. Test the internal temperature with an instant-read thermometer. It should read at least 160°F (71°C) in the thickest part of the breast.

6 Transfer the chicken to a serving platter or rimmed baking sheet. Carve and serve. Drizzle some of the cooking juices over the cut chicken.

Indian "Butter" Chicken

There are very few healthy meals of which my kids, of their own accord, will eat three helpings and tell me over and over how much they love it. Indian butter chicken is one of those recipes. It's great for families and for expanding the palates of young (or older, more hesitant) eaters. They'll be won over by its rich, complex tomato gravy that surrounds tender chicken pieces.

Prep time 15 minutes

Pressure time 10 minutes + 5 minutes natural release

Serves 6

4 tablespoons (60 ml) ghee (page 234) or (55 g) grass-fed butter

1 tablespoon (10 g) minced garlic

1 tablespoon (6 g) minced ginger

1 cup (235 ml) tomato sauce

2 tablespoons (32 g) tomato paste

1 tablespoon (5 g) dried minced onion

1 tablespoon (6 g) ground coriander

1 tablespoon (7 g) garam masala, divided

1 tablespoon (7 g) sweet paprika

1 teaspoon ground turmeric

1 teaspoon ground cumin

1 teaspoon sea salt

2 pounds (900 g) chicken breasts or thighs, cut into 1-inch (2.5 cm) pieces

1 cup (235 ml) full-fat coconut milk

Roasted Cauliflower Rice (page 200) or squash noodles, for serving

1 Turn your cooker to the medium sauté setting. Add the ghee. When the pot is preheated, add the garlic and ginger. Cook for 1 minute.

2 Add the tomato sauce, tomato paste, dried minced onion, coriander, 2 teaspoons of the garam masala, paprika, turmeric, cumin, and salt. Cook for 2–3 minutes.

3 Add the chicken pieces to the pot and stir to coat everything.

4 Place the lid on your cooker, close the steam valve, and set it to cook on high pressure for 10 minutes. Let the cooker release the pressure naturally for at least 5 minutes. After this, you can release the remaining pressure manually or let it release on its own.

5 Stir in the coconut milk and the remaining 1 teaspoon (2 g) of garam masala. If it needs to be heated more, turn it to the sauté setting and heat until bubbly again.

6 Serve with your desired side dish.

Notes:

- *Garam masala is an Indian spice blend found in most grocery stores in the spice section.*
- *I highly recommend serving this with some of the paleo tzatziki from the Gyro-Inspired Shredded Beef and Tzatziki Sauce recipe (page 105), replacing the fresh herbs with fresh chopped cilantro.*

BBQ Ranch Chicken Bites with Roasted Sweet Potatoes

I admit, this recipe could be easily made in a skillet on the stovetop, but I prefer using my pressure cooker because it does a better job of tenderizing the chicken. And can I just tell you how much I love BBQ sauce and ranch mixed together? Especially with chicken. And sweet potato fries. This meal has so many of my favorite things in it!

Prep time 20 minutes

Pressure time 3 minutes + 20-25 minutes roasting time

Serves 6

Recommended side: green salad

Note: The spice blend that is on the sweet potato fries is the Sweet Potato Fry Seasoning from my website, perrysplate.com. I keep a large mason jar of it in the pantry and use it all the time for more than just sweet potato fries!

2-2½ pounds (900-1135 g) sweet potatoes, peeled and cut into ½-inch (1.3 cm) cubes or into fries

6 tablespoons (90 ml) avocado oil, divided

1 teaspoon sea salt

1 teaspoon chili powder

1 teaspoon garlic powder or granulated garlic

1 teaspoon ground cumin

2 pounds (900 g) boneless, skinless chicken breasts or thighs, cut into 1-inch (2.5 cm) chunks

1 cup (235 ml) paleo-friendly BBQ sauce (like the Smoky Maple BBQ Sauce on page 239), divided

½ cup (120 ml) Paleo-Friendly Ranch Dressing (page 237), divided

1 Preheat your oven to 425°F (220°C, or gas mark 7).

2 Spread the sweet potato cubes on two rimmed baking sheets. Drizzle 1 tablespoon (15 ml) of the avocado oil on each baking sheet.

3 Combine the salt, chili powder, garlic powder, and cumin in a small bowl. Sprinkle 1½ teaspoons of seasoning over each pan of potatoes. Use your hands to toss the potatoes and coat them in the oil and spices. Put the pans in the oven and roast for 20-25 minutes, rotating the pans halfway through and flipping the potatoes around once or twice. They should be deeply browned in spots and soft in the centers.

4 Meanwhile, turn the cooker to high sauté and add 2 tablespoons (28 ml) of avocado oil to the pot. Sprinkle the remaining 1 teaspoon of seasoning on the chicken pieces. When the pot has preheated, add half of the chicken to the pot and sear for 3-4 minutes, flipping them around once during cooking. Remove the chicken, add the remaining 2 tablespoons (28 ml) of avocado oil and sear the rest of the chicken.

5 Return all of the chicken to the pot and add ½ cup (120 ml) of the BBQ sauce to the pot. Stir and then close the lid and the steam valve. Set the cooker to high pressure for 3 minutes and then use a quick release to manually release the pressure.

6 Add ¼ cup (60 ml) of BBQ sauce and ¼ cup (60 ml) of the Paleo-Friendly Ranch Dressing to the pot. This should create a nice, flavorful sauce. Add a little more of the remaining ¼ cup (60 ml) of BBQ sauce or dressing, depending on your preference.

7 Serve the chicken bites with the sauce and a helping of roasted sweet potatoes.

Chicken Alfredo with Broccoli and Leeks

This recipe is so creamy and rich-tasting you'll feel like it's an indulgence, but at the same time, it's light and won't leave you feeling heavy like dairy-based Alfredo sauce does. I love the way the broccoli kind of breaks down and becomes part of the sauce—like a cheesy broccoli soup sauce.

Prep time 10 minutes
Pressure time 4 minutes
Serves 6

2 tablespoons (28 ml) ghee (page 234) or grass-fed butter

2 leeks, medium and darker green parts trimmed off and the rest chopped

2 teaspoons minced garlic

1 teaspoon sea salt

2–2½ pounds (900–1135 g) boneless skinless chicken breast or thigh meat, cut into 1-inch (2.5 cm) pieces

½ teaspoon dried thyme

½ teaspoon dried basil

2 tablespoons (28 ml) freshly squeezed lemon juice

¼ cup (60 ml) chicken broth, homemade (page 242) or store-bought

1½ pounds (680 g) broccoli florets

2 cups (475 ml) Garlic Alfredo Sauce (page 240), divided

1 Put the ghee in the pot and set the cooker to high sauté. When it has preheated, add the leeks and cook for 3-4 minutes until they have softened. Add the garlic to the pot and turn the cooker off.

2 Sprinkle the salt on the chicken and add it to the pot along with the thyme, basil, lemon juice, and chicken broth.

3 Close the lid and the steam valve. Set the cooker to high pressure for 3 minutes. Release the pressure manually. Add the broccoli and repressurize the cooker for another minute. Do a quick release when the broccoli is finished

4 Add 1½ cups (355 ml) of the Alfredo sauce to the pot and stir it around. If you feel it needs more, add the remaining ½ cup (120 ml).

Recommended sides: squash noodles or Basic Spaghetti Squash (page 194)

Chicken Cordon Bleu with Creamy Garlic Sauce

I wanted to re-create a version of chicken cordon bleu because it was one of my favorite dishes for years. I felt like I did the classic version justice with the creamy, paleo-friendly Alfredo sauce that gets drizzled over the top at the end.

Prep time: 15 minutes

Pressure time: 8 minutes + 5 minutes natural release

Serves 6

Six 8-ounce (225 g) boneless, skinless chicken breasts

Sea salt

Dried thyme

6 thin slices of deli ham

3 tablespoons (45 g) Dijon mustard, divided

½ cup (120 ml) chicken broth, homemade (page 242) or store-bought

⅔ cup (160 ml) Garlic Alfredo Sauce (page 240)

1 teaspoon tapioca flour (optional)

¼ cup (60 ml) water (optional)

1 Lay a sheet of plastic wrap on a flat work surface. Lay one or two chicken breasts on the plastic and then cover the chicken with another large piece of plastic wrap. Whack the chicken with a meat tenderizer or a rolling pin until flattened to ½ inch (1.3 cm) thick. Repeat with the other chicken breasts.

2 Assemble the chicken rolls by sprinkling one side of the chicken with a pinch of salt and dried thyme. Lay a piece of deli ham on the chicken and spread with ½ teaspoon of the Dijon mustard. Start on one end and roll the chicken and ham together. Secure with a toothpick. Place the chicken roll in the pot. (No rack needed.)

3 Repeat with the remaining chicken and nestle all of the rolls snugly in the pot. Sprinkle a pinch of salt and dried thyme over each chicken roll and pour the chicken broth down the side of the pot.

4 Close the lid and the steam valve. Set the cooker to high pressure for 8 minutes. Let the cooker release pressure on its own for 5 minutes before manually releasing the rest of the pressure.

5 Transfer the chicken rolls to a serving platter and cover to keep warm.

6 Turn the cooker to medium sauté. Add the remaining 2 tablespoons (30 g) of Dijon mustard and the Garlic Alfredo Sauce to the cooking juices in the pot. Whisk and heat until bubbly. If the sauce is too thin for your liking, mix the tapioca flour with the water and slowly drizzle it into the sauce while whisking. That should thicken it up well. Taste and add a pinch or two of salt, if needed.

7 Serve the cordon bleu rolls with a few spoonfuls of sauce.

Shredded Red Curry Chicken and Sweet Thai Slaw

This recipe is one of the most popular pressure cooker recipes from my website, Perry's Plate. I felt like it needed a home here in this book, too. Store-bought curry paste is one of my favorite shortcuts because it has all of the hard-to-find ingredients common to Thai cuisine. Most curry pastes I've seen are pretty clean, but be sure to check the ingredient label anyway for things you might not want added to your meal.

Prep time   20 minutes

Pressure time   25 minutes + 10 minutes natural release

Serves   8-10

For the chicken:

3 pounds (1.4 kg) boneless, skinless chicken thighs or breasts

3 tablespoons (45 g) red curry paste

2 tablespoons (28 ml) coconut aminos

4 tablespoons (60 ml) lime juice (about 2 limes), divided

1 tablespoon (15 ml) fish sauce

1 teaspoon salt

One 13.5-ounce (385 g) can coconut milk

For the slaw:

1 medium head of cabbage, either green or red, shredded

3 scallions, sliced

2 tablespoons (28 ml) lime juice (about 1 lime)

2 tablespoons (28 ml) avocado oil

2 teaspoons honey

1 teaspoon fish sauce

½-1 teaspoon sambal oelek or Asian chili garlic paste, plus more for serving

½ teaspoon sea salt

Lime wedges, for serving

1 To make the chicken, place the chicken in the pot.

2 Whisk together the curry paste, coconut aminos, 2 tablespoons (28 ml) of the lime juice, fish sauce, and salt. Pour the mixture over the chicken and move and flip the chicken around with a pair of tongs to coat it well.

3 Close the lid and steam valve and set it to high pressure for 25 minutes.

4 Meanwhile, make the slaw by putting the shredded cabbage and scallions in a large salad bowl.

5 Whisk together the 2 tablespoons (28 ml) of lime juice, avocado oil, honey, fish sauce, sambal oelek, and salt. Pour it over the cabbage and toss to combine. Chill until ready to serve.

6 When the chicken is finished cooking, let the cooker release pressure naturally for 10 minutes before releasing the rest of the pressure manually.

7 Shred the chicken inside the pot and stir in the coconut milk and remaining 2 tablespoons (28 ml) of lime juice. Taste and add additional salt, if needed. At this point, you can also stir in a spoonful or two of sambal oelek if you'd like it spicier.

8 Serve the chicken over a bed of the slaw alongside additional sambal oelek and lime wedges.

Pizza-Stuffed Chicken with Marinara Sauce

When I started playing with pizza "flavored" dishes, I realized that my favorite parts of pizza are actually the toppings and sauce. (And cheese, but am I allowed to admit that here?) Stuffing some of my favorite pizza toppings into a chicken breast and covering it with marinara is such a delicious way to get all of those tasty pizza flavors without needing a crust.

Prep time 15 minutes

Pressure time 8 minutes + 5 minutes natural release

Serves 6

6 small to medium chicken breasts

1 tablespoon (4 g) nutritional yeast

¾ teaspoon dried oregano

¾ teaspoon garlic powder

½ teaspoon sea salt

12 pepperoni slices

½ cup (75 g) diced ham

¼ cup (35 g) sliced black olives

¼ cup (25 g) peperoncini slices

One 32-ounce (905 g) jar marinara sauce, divided

1 Cut a slit horizontally into the thick sides of the chicken breasts—about three-fourths of the way through, so you can almost open it like a book.

2 In a small bowl, combine the nutritional yeast, oregano, garlic powder, and salt. Sprinkle the mixture on the outside of the chicken and inside the slits.

3 Divide the pepperoni, ham, olives, and peperoncini slices into the slits in the chicken. Put the stuffed chicken into the pot. (No rack needed.) Pour 1½ cups (355 ml) of the marinara sauce over the top of the chicken. Lift a few of the chicken pieces so the marinara can run down underneath.

4 Close the lid and the steam valve. Set the cooker to high pressure for 8 minutes. Let the cooker release pressure naturally for 5 minutes and then release the rest of the pressure.

5 While the chicken is cooking, heat the rest of the marinara sauce in a small saucepan.

6 Serve the stuffed chicken breasts with warm marinara sauce.

Shredded Chipotle Salsa Chicken

I was surprised at how much we all loved this chicken! It's so simple and is one of those examples of something being more than the sum of its parts. The chipotle pepper is a key ingredient here, but if you can't find canned chipotle peppers, you can use ½–1 teaspoon of dried chipotle pepper powder. (It's pretty spicy, so use with caution.) Serve in tacos, on taco salads, in rice bowls, added to soups, or on your morning hash!

Prep time 10 minutes

Pressure time 15 minutes + 15 minutes natural release

Serves 8-10

3 pounds (1.4 kg) boneless, skinless chicken breasts or thighs

1½ cups (390 g) salsa

1 chipotle, from a can of chipotles in adobo sauce, minced

1 tablespoon (16 g) tomato paste

1 juicy lime

½ cup (8 g) chopped fresh cilantro

1 Put the chicken in the pot. Whisk together the salsa, minced chipotle pepper, tomato paste, and the juice from half of the lime. Pour the mixture over the chicken.

2 Close the lid and the steam valve. Set the cooker to high pressure for 15 minutes. Let the cooker release pressure on its own for 15 minutes and then manually release any remaining pressure.

3 Remove the chicken from the pot and shred it with a couple of forks. Return the shredded chicken to the pot and stir in the cilantro and the juice from the other half of the lime.

Italian Peperoncini Shredded Chicken

I can't believe I used to be the girl who would intentionally avoid getting a peperoncini pepper when I served myself out of the Olive Garden salad bowl. I love them so much now! They're a perfect little spicy bite mixed with this Italian-style shredded chicken.

Prep time 15 minutes

Pressure time 20 minutes + 15 minutes natural release

Serves 6

3 pounds (1.4 kg) boneless, skinless chicken breasts or thighs

Juice from ½ large lemon (about 3 tablespoons [45 ml])

4 teaspoons (8 g) Italian seasoning

1 tablespoon (10 g) minced garlic (about 4 large cloves)

1½ teaspoons sea salt (see note)

½ cup (50 g) sliced peperoncini peppers, drained

½ cup (120 ml) chicken broth, homemade (page 242) or store-bought

1 Put the chicken in the pot. Sprinkle the lemon juice, Italian seasoning, garlic, and salt over the chicken. Use a pair of tongs to toss the chicken around to coat it evenly in the seasonings.

2 Add the peperoncini peppers on top of the chicken. Pour the chicken broth down the side of the pot.

3 Close the lid and the steam valve. Set the cooker to high pressure for 20 minutes. Let the cooker release pressure naturally for 15 minutes before releasing any remaining pressure manually.

4 Transfer the chicken to a serving platter (leave the juices in the pot), shred it into bite-size pieces, and return it to the pot. Toss the chicken around to soak up some of the juices.

Note: If your Italian seasoning happens to have salt, you may want to cut the salt measurement in half.

Recommended sides: As a salad atop a bed of lettuce (or lettuce wrap) with artichoke hearts, sun-dried tomatoes, and a light vinaigrette; or alongside some herbed roasted vegetables (like asparagus, broccoli, cauliflower, and Brussels sprouts)

Lemon-Garlic Chicken Thighs and Artichokes

I find that chicken thighs are much more forgiving and harder to overcook than chicken breasts. I love how juicy and richer-tasting they are! If you're not a fan of dark chicken meat, you can also use breast meat in this recipe.

Prep time 10 minutes
Pressure time 9 minutes
Serves 6

6 boneless, skinless chicken thighs

Sea salt and black pepper

Zest and juice of 1 lemon (keep separate)

2 tablespoons (28 ml) ghee (page 234) or avocado oil

1 shallot, diced

2 teaspoons (6 g) minced garlic

½ cup (120 ml) chicken broth, homemade (page 242) or store-bought

½ teaspoon dried thyme

One 14-ounce (352 g) jar artichoke hearts (in water or olive oil), drained

2 tablespoons (28 ml) coconut cream (optional)

1 Sprinkle the chicken thighs on both sides with a few generous pinches of salt and pepper. Squeeze the juice from half of the lemon over the chicken.

2 Turn your cooker to the high sauté setting and add the ghee to the pot. When it has preheated, sear the thighs in two batches, forming golden brown crusts on both sides of each thigh. Transfer the thighs to a large plate when they are finished searing. They do not have to be cooked all the way through at this point.

3 Add the shallots and garlic to the pot and sauté for 3-4 minutes until the shallots are tender. Add the chicken broth to the pot and scrape up any browned bits that are stuck to the bottom of the pot.

4 Return the thighs to the pot along with the thyme and a couple pinches of lemon zest and the juice from the other half of the lemon.

5 Close the lid and the steam valve. Set it to high pressure for 9 minutes. Release the pressure manually when it has finished cooking.

6 Open the pot and transfer the chicken to a serving platter. Cover the chicken to keep it warm. Turn the pot to the high sauté setting and add the drained artichoke hearts and coconut cream (if using). Stir and let it simmer for 5 minutes until everything is heated through and the sauce has reduced a bit and thickened.

Recommended sides: squash noodles, Roasted Cauliflower Rice (page 200), or roasted potatoes

Coconut-Lime Chicken Thighs

Coconut and lime is such a fantastic flavor combination for chicken. This chicken stands alone well with a simple side dish or you could turn it into a pretty fabulous chicken taco salad. Just sayin'.

Prep time 15 minutes
Pressure time 8 minutes
Serves 6

½ teaspoon sea salt
6 boneless, skinless chicken thighs
2 tablespoons (28 ml) avocado oil, divided
2 limes

2 tablespoons (28 ml) coconut aminos
1 teaspoon minced garlic
1 teaspoon dried minced onion
Pinch of crushed red pepper flakes
1 cup (235 ml) coconut milk

1 Sprinkle the salt over both sides of the chicken thighs.

2 Put 1 tablespoon (15 ml) of the avocado oil in the pot and set the cooker to high sauté.

3 Sear the chicken in two batches, adding the remaining 1 tablespoon (15 ml) of avocado oil between batches, until a golden crust forms on each side. Return the chicken to the pot and turn the cooker off.

4 Combine the zest from 1 lime and juice from both limes, coconut aminos, garlic, dried minced onion, and red pepper flakes in a small bowl. Pour the sauce over the chicken.

5 Close the lid and the steam valve. Set the cooker to high pressure for 8 minutes. Release the pressure manually when it finishes cooking.

6 Transfer the chicken to a serving platter (leave the juices in the pot) and cover to keep warm.

7 Add the coconut milk to the pot and turn the cooker to high sauté. Simmer for 5 minutes or until the sauce has reduced some.

8 Pour the sauce over the chicken and serve with desired side dish.

Recommended side dishes: Roasted Cauliflower Rice (page 200), squash noodles, or Whole Steamed Potatoes (page 183)

Creamy Chicken Thighs and Mushrooms

I feel like dried mushrooms are a powerful secret ingredient—especially if the mushrooms are a mixed variety. It gives this chicken and gravy dish more depth, and an extra punch of mushroom flavor is never a bad thing.

Prep time 15 minutes

Pressure time 9

Serves 8

Recommended sides: steamed rice, squash noodles, or mashed potatoes

2 tablespoons (28 ml) avocado oil, divided

8 boneless, skinless chicken thighs

1 teaspoon sea salt

1 teaspoon dried thyme

¼ teaspoon black pepper

Juice from ½ lemon (1–2 tablespoons [15–28 ml])

1 cup (160 g) diced sweet onion

8 ounces (225 g) sliced brown mushrooms

1 cup (50 g) dried mixed mushrooms (or 8 more ounces [225 g] of a different kind of mushroom)

2 teaspoons minced garlic

½ cup (120 ml) chicken broth, home-made (page 242) or store-bought

3 tablespoons (45 ml) coconut aminos

⅓ cup (80 ml) full-fat coconut milk

2 tablespoons (16 g) tapioca or (18 g) arrowroot flour

2 teaspoons red wine vinegar

1 Turn the cooker to the high sauté setting and add 1 tablespoon (15 ml) of the avocado oil to the pot.

2 Sprinkle the thighs with the salt, thyme, and pepper. Drizzle the lemon juice over the chicken.

3 When the cooker has preheated fully, put four of the thighs into the pot. Cook for 2–3 minutes and then flip, to form a light golden crust on both sides. Remove the thighs, add the remaining 1 tablespoon (15 ml) of avocado oil to the pot, and add the remaining four thighs. Cook to form a light golden crust on both sides and then remove those thighs and set aside with the others.

4 Add the onion to the pot and cook for 2–3 minutes until they begin to soften. Add the sliced mushrooms, dried mushrooms, garlic, chicken broth, and coconut aminos to the pot.

5 Return the chicken thighs to the pot and nestle them in with the mushroom mixture. Close the lid and the steam valve. Set the cooker to high pressure for 9 minutes. Use a quick release to manually release all of the pressure.

6 Transfer the chicken to a serving platter and cover to keep warm. Leave the mushroom sauce in the pot. Turn the cooker to the high sauté setting. Whisk together the coconut milk and tapioca flour and pour it into the pot while stirring the sauce. Cook for 2–3 minutes until the sauce is bubbly. Stir in the red wine vinegar, and then taste and add a little more vinegar or some salt, if necessary.

7 Return the chicken to the pot and serve with the sauce.

Chile-Lime Drumsticks with Braised Cabbage

This recipe uses one of my favorite spice blends that I created—the Chorizo Seasoning (page 243). I created that blend when I was attempting a knockoff recipe of the pork and chicken chorizo from Chipotle. I ended up with a seasoning blend that not only makes amazing homemade chorizo but also works well on any type of meat or to anything you want to give a Tex-Mex flavor. It's like taco seasoning's cooler, younger brother.

Prep time 15 minutes + marinating time

Pressure time: 22 minutes + 5 minutes natural release + 5 minutes broil

Serves 5

10 chicken drumsticks

4 teaspoons (8 g) Chorizo Seasoning (page 243)

Zest and juice of 1 large juicy lime

1 teaspoon sea salt

½ cup (120 ml) chicken broth, homemade (page 242) or store-bought

1 small head of cabbage (1½–2 pounds [455–680 g])

½ cup (8 g) chopped fresh cilantro

Diced avocado or guacamole, for serving

1 Put the drumsticks in a large bowl. Combine the Chorizo Seasoning, the zest from the whole lime, the juice from ½ of the lime, and the salt to form a paste. Pour it over the chicken and use your hands to toss everything together until the chicken is well coated in the spice mixture. Cover the bowl with plastic wrap and chill for at least 4 hours or up to 24 hours.

2 When you're ready to cook the chicken, prepare the cooker by putting the wire rack in the pot with the chicken broth. Arrange the drumsticks vertically on the rack, meaty-sides down. The bony ends will lean up against the pot.

3 Close the lid and the steam valve. Set the cooker to high pressure for 18 minutes. Let the cooker release pressure naturally for 5 minutes and then release the rest of the pressure manually.

4 Meanwhile, turn the oven broiler on high and line a baking sheet with aluminum foil. Cut the cabbage head in half, cut out the core, and chop the whole thing into bite-size pieces.

5 Transfer the chicken to the prepared baking sheet. Before putting the chicken in the oven, put the cabbage in the pot. Close the lid and the steam valve and set the cooker to high pressure for 4 minutes.

6 When the cooker repressurizes, put the chicken under the broiler on the top rack for about 5 minutes until the skin crisps up. It should be done around the same time as the cabbage—just do a manual pressure release and toss the cabbage around in the juices before transferring it to a serving platter with the chicken. Squeeze the juice from the other half of the lime over the chicken and cabbage and sprinkle with the cilantro and a pinch of salt.

7 Serve with diced avocado or guacamole.

Chicken Drumsticks with Tangy Bacon and Mustard Sauce

Up until now, I had a tricky relationship with drumsticks. I liked having a piece of chicken with a built-in handle, but I had a hard time getting them tender. Enter: Pressure Cooker. Friends, this is the missing piece. The pressure cooker tenderizes these portable pieces of chicken like no other. And just a quick broil in the oven will crisp up the skin and finish them off.

Prep time 20 minutes

Pressure time 15 minutes +
5 minutes natural release + 5-10 minutes broiling time

Serves 4

10 ounces (280 g) thick-cut bacon, cut into ½-inch (1.3 cm) pieces
1¼ cups (295 ml) water, divided
8 chicken drumsticks
1 teaspoon sea salt
1 teaspoon onion powder
½ teaspoon paprika
¼ teaspoon black pepper
2 tablespoons (30 g) whole-grain mustard, divided
1 tablespoon (8 g) tapioca flour
½ lemon

1 Turn the cooker to the high sauté setting and add the bacon to the pot. Cook, stirring often, until crispy, about 15 minutes. Turn off the cooker.

2 Remove the bacon from the pot and set aside for later. Drain all but 2–3 tablespoons (28–45 ml) of the bacon drippings. Add 1 cup (235 ml) of the water to the pot as well as the wire rack.

3 Meanwhile, sprinkle the drumsticks with the salt, onion powder, paprika, pepper, and 1 tablespoon (15 g) of the mustard. Use your hands to coat the chicken in the mixture.

4 Put the chicken legs in the pot standing upright, meat-side down, and leaning against the side of the pot. Close the lid and the steam valve. Set the cooker to high pressure for 15 minutes. Let the cooker release pressure naturally for 5 minutes and then manually release the rest of the pressure.

5 Turn your oven broiler on high and line a rimmed baking sheet with aluminum foil.

6 When the chicken is finished cooking, transfer the legs to the prepared baking sheet and broil for 5-10 minutes to crisp up the skin a little.

7 Meanwhile, whisk together the remaining ¼ cup (60 ml) water and the tapioca flour. Remove the wire rack from the pot and turn it to the high sauté setting. While whisking, pour in the tapioca slurry and simmer for 2–3 minutes until the mixture has thickened slightly. Turn off the heat and stir in the reserved bacon and the remaining 1 tablespoon (15 g) of mustard. Squeeze a little of the juice from the lemon half into the sauce. Taste and add more lemon or a pinch of salt if you think it needs it.

8 Serve the chicken legs with the bacon and mustard sauce.

Roasted Ratatouille Turkey Meatloaf and Marinara

This is one of those recipes that blew me away with flavor and exceeded my expectations. I love the roasted vegetable and pancetta mixture so much that I sometimes make a big batch of it over the weekend and add it to my morning eggs during the week.

Prep time 30 minutes

Pressure time 15 minutes + 5 minutes natural release

Serves 5

1 small zucchini, cut into ½-inch (1.3 cm) pieces

2 cups (164 g) diced eggplant, cut into ½-inch (1.3 cm) pieces

6 ounces (170 g) quartered cherry or grape tomatoes

1 shallot, chopped

4 ounces (115 g) diced pancetta or bacon

2 tablespoons (28 ml) avocado oil

¾ teaspoon sea salt, plus more for seasoning

1 pound (455 g) ground turkey

2 tablespoons (28 ml) red wine vinegar

1 tablespoon (10 g) minced garlic

1 teaspoon herbes de Provence or Italian seasoning

Pinch of crushed red pepper flakes

1 tablespoon (15 ml) ghee (page 234) or (14 g) grass-fed butter

One 24-ounce (680 g) jar marinara sauce

1 Turn on your oven broiler and place an oven rack 4–5 inches (10–13 cm) from the heating element.

2 Place the zucchini, eggplant, tomatoes, shallot, and pancetta on a large rimmed baking sheet. Drizzle the avocado oil over the top, use your hands to toss everything around, and then spread it around evenly on the baking sheet. Sprinkle with a couple generous pinches of salt. Broil for about 15 minutes, turning everything a couple of times during cooking, until the vegetables have dark golden brown spots.

3 Prepare the cooker by pouring 1½ cups (355 ml) of water in the bottom of the pot and placing the wire rack inside. Tear off two sheets of aluminum foil about 18 inches (46 cm) long. Fold each in half lengthwise, then in half again lengthwise to form a long strip. Place each strip into the cooker, forming an x-shaped "sling."

4 Place the turkey in a large bowl. Add the vinegar, garlic, seasoning, ¾ teaspoon of salt, and red pepper flakes. When the roasted vegetables and pancetta are finished and have cooled some, add them to the turkey. Use your hands to gently mix everything together. Form the meat into a giant, round pancake shape, no more than 2 inches (5 cm) thick.

5 Lay the meat in the center of the foil sling. Drizzle the ghee over the top of the meat.

6 Close the lid and the steam valve. Set the cooker to high pressure for 15 minutes. Let the cooker release the pressure on its own for 5 minutes and then release the rest of the pressure manually.

7 Warm the marinara sauce in a saucepan.

8 Transfer the meatloaf to a serving dish, slice, and top with the warm marinara sauce.

Tahini and Pine Nut Meatballs with Spiced Tomato Sauce

This is a Middle Eastern take on meatballs and marinara with a lightly spiced sauce. The meatballs freeze beautifully, too! After searing, freeze them on a cookie sheet and, when frozen, transfer them to a freezer-safe container. Just add the frozen meatballs to the pressure cooker after you make the sauce in step 3 and add an extra minute of pressurizing time.

Prep time 20 minutes

Pressure time 5 minutes + 5 minutes natural release

Makes about 25 meatballs

Recommended side dishes: Cauliflower Puree with Rosemary and Garlic (page 201), Roasted Cauliflower Rice (page 200), Basic Spaghetti Squash (page 194), or squash noodles

Note: I like to use a combination of turkey and pork because pork adds some fat to keep the turkey from drying out, and the flavor of the meat remains neutral. Beef is great too, but it has a stronger flavor.

For the meatballs:

2 pounds (900 g) ground turkey or pork (or a combination of the two)

4 teaspoons (15 g) Middle Eastern Seasoning (page 245)

4 teaspoons (12 g) minced garlic

½ cup (68 g) pine nuts, toasted

⅓ cup (80 g) tahini

1 teaspoon sea salt

4 tablespoons (60 ml) avocado oil, divided

For the sauce:

1 cup (160 g) chopped sweet onion

½ teaspoon ground cumin

½ teaspoon ground coriander

Pinch of ground cinnamon

One 14-ounce (395 g) can diced tomatoes

½ teaspoon minced garlic

1 tablespoon (16 g) tomato paste

½ cup (120 ml) chicken broth, homemade (page 242) or store-bought

¼ cup (15 g) chopped fresh parsley

¼ cup (24 g) chopped fresh mint

1 lemon

1 To make the meatballs, place the meat into a medium bowl. Add the Middle Eastern Seasoning, garlic, pine nuts, tahini, and salt. Use your hands to gently mix everything together thoroughly. Roll the meat into tight, 1½-inch (3.8 cm) meatballs.

2 Turn the cooker to the high sauté setting and add 2 tablespoons (28 ml) of the avocado oil to the pot. When it has preheated, sear half of the meatballs on both sides, letting each side cook undisturbed for 3–4 minutes until a golden crust has formed. Add the remaining 2 tablespoons (28 ml) of avocado oil and sear the second batch of meatballs. They don't have to be cooked through at this point. Transfer the meatballs to a plate.

3 To make the sauce, add the onion, cumin, coriander, and cinnamon to the pot. Cook for 1–2 minutes and then add the tomatoes, garlic, tomato paste, and chicken broth, stirring well to incorporate the tomato paste.

4 Return the meatballs to the pot. Close the lid and the steam valve. Set the cooker to high pressure for 5 minutes. Let the pressure release naturally for 5 minutes and then manually release the rest of the pressure.

5 Sprinkle the fresh herbs over the meatballs and sauce and squeeze some lemon juice over the top. Serve with your choice of side dish.

6

PERFECT PORK

I love the way a big pork roast seems to melt and fall apart in juicy, tender threads after a ride in a pressure cooker. It never gets old for me. Luckily, ribs, loin roasts, and pork loin stews turn out flavorful and tender as well. The hardest part is figuring out which cut to use for dinner.

Recipes

Mango BBQ Pulled Pork

BBQ pulled pork is such a great recipe to have in your repertoire! It seems to please the general meat-eating population, and it's easy to make a batch large enough to serve a crowd. You can also make a more traditional BBQ pulled pork using my Smoky Maple BBQ Sauce (page 239) and omitting the mango.

Prep time 15 minutes

Pressure time 60 minutes + 15 minutes natural release

Serves 10

One 4- to 5-pound (1.8–2.3 kg) pork shoulder roast

2 tablespoons (20 g) steak seasoning

1 teaspoon sea salt

2 tablespoons (28 ml) bacon drippings, ghee (page 234), or avocado oil

1½ cups (240 g) chopped sweet onion

1 tablespoon (10 g) minced garlic

2–3 cups (475–700 ml) Mango-Chile BBQ Sauce (page 239), divided

1 lemon

1 cup (175 g) diced mango, cut into ½-inch (1.3 cm) pieces

1 Cut the roast into 4 roughly equal pieces. Sprinkle the steak seasoning and salt all over the roast pieces.

2 Put your fat of choice in the pot and set the cooker to the high sauté setting. When it has preheated, sear the roast chunks, in batches if necessary, until a golden crust forms on a couple of sides of each piece.

3 Add the onion, garlic, and 1 cup (235 ml) of the BBQ sauce on top of the pork.

4 Close the lid and the steam valve. Set the cooker to high pressure for 60 minutes. Let the pressure release naturally or at least for 15 minutes before releasing it manually.

5 Remove the pork from the pot and shred it. Remove the liquid from the pot and set aside. Return the shredded pork to the pot with the remaining 1–2 cups (235–475 ml) of BBQ sauce. Toss to coat evenly. Add a little of the pot juices back to the pot if it seems too dry, but don't add too much or the pork will be watery.

6 Squeeze the juice from half of the lemon on the pork and stir in the chopped mango. Taste and add more lemon or salt, if needed.

Recommended sides: Whole Steamed Sweet Potato (page 183), Roasted Cauliflower Rice (page 200), or Basic Spaghetti Squash (page 194)

Caribbean Pineapple Pulled Pork

You can't have too many pulled pork recipes. Truly. Pork isn't a one-trick pony and will pair well with just about any flavors you throw at it. I love the combination of pineapple and pork with some heat. This island-style pulled pork is a fun twist on traditional pulled pork.

Prep time 15 minutes
Pressure time 60 minutes + 15 minutes natural release
Serves 8-10

One 3- to 4-pound (1.4–1.8 kg) pork shoulder roast

1½ teaspoon sea salt

2 tablespoons (32 g) jerk seasoning blend

2 limes

2 tablespoons (20 g) minced garlic

2 tablespoons (16 g) grated ginger

1½ cups (248 g) fresh pineapple chunks

2 tablespoons (40 g) molasses

⅛ teaspoon crushed red pepper flakes

½ cup (120 ml) chicken broth, homemade (page 242) or store-bought

1 cup (235 ml) coconut milk

1 Cut the roast into 3–4 roughly equally sized pieces. Rub the meat with the salt and the jerk seasoning blend. Place the pieces in the pot.

2 Add the zest from 1 of the limes, the juice from both of the limes, garlic, ginger, pineapple chunks, molasses, red pepper flakes, and chicken broth.

3 Close the lid and the steam valve. Set the cooker to high pressure for 60 minutes. Let the cooker release the pressure naturally for at least 15 minutes before releasing it manually.

4 Remove the pork from the pot, shred it, and return it to the pot. Stir in the coconut milk.

Recommended sides: Roasted Cauliflower Rice (page 200) or Whole Steamed Sweet Potatoes (page 183)

Cajun Pulled Pork with Andouille Sausage

Using two kinds of pork in a recipe is OK, right? Actually, don't tell me if it isn't. This bold pulled pork with spicy bits of andouille is too good not to make.

Prep time 20 minutes

Pressure time 60 minutes + 15 minutes natural release

Serves 8–10

1 tablespoon (15 ml) avocado oil

1½ cups (240 g) diced sweet onion

2 celery stalks, diced

½ green bell pepper, seeded and diced

1 tablespoon (10 g) minced garlic

One 3-pound (1.4 kg) pork shoulder roast

1 teaspoon sea salt

1 tablespoon (9 g) Cajun seasoning

One 8-ounce (225 g) can tomato sauce

¼ cup (60 ml) red wine vinegar

5–6 ounces (140–170 g) andouille sausage (2–3 links)

1 Turn the cooker to the high sauté setting and add the avocado oil. When the pot has preheated, add the onion, celery, and green pepper. Cook, stirring often, until the vegetables have softened, about 5 minutes. Stir in the garlic and turn the cooker off.

2 Cut the roast in half and rub the salt and Cajun seasoning over all the sides of the meat. Add the meat to the pot. Pour the tomato sauce and vinegar over the top.

3 Close the lid and the steam valve. Set the cooker to high pressure for 60 minutes. Let the cooker release the pressure naturally for at least 15 minutes before releasing it manually.

4 A few minutes before the pork is finished, put the sausages into a skillet and cook over medium heat until mostly heated through and golden brown on the outside.

5 When the pork is finished, remove the meat from the pot, shred it, and then return it to the pot. Dice the sausage and add it to the pot as well.

Recommended sides: Roasted Cauliflower Rice (page 200), Whole Steamed Potatoes (page 183), or shredded cabbage tossed in a little lime juice and avocado oil

Easy Carnitas for a Crowd

There are two reasons why this recipe will be your go-to carnitas recipe from now on. First, it's so easy with just a handful of ingredients and much quicker in a pressure cooker. Second, oven-frying the cooked pulled pork makes it easier to feed a crowd and using bacon drippings is somewhat life-altering. Also, my method for frying can also be used to make the best shredded hash browns of your life. Was that three reasons?

Prep time 20 minutes

Pressure time 120 minutes + 15 minutes natural release + 10-15 minutes roasting time

Serves 10-12

2 tablespoons (30 g) sea salt

One 7- to 8-pound (3.2–3.6 kg) boneless pork shoulder roast, cut into 4–5 pieces

½ cup (120 ml) bacon drippings or avocado oil, divided

2 cups (475 ml) water

Juice from 1 orange

2 limes, divided

4 bay leaves

6 cloves of garlic, smashed

1 Sprinkle the salt over the roast pieces.

2 Turn the cooker to the high sauté setting. Add 2 tablespoons (28 ml) of the bacon drippings to the pot. When it has preheated, sear two pieces of the roast at a time on two sides until a golden crust forms, about 2–3 minutes on each side. Repeat with the other pieces of roast and 2 tablespoons (28 ml) of bacon drippings.

3 Turn off the cooker. Return all of the pork to the pot and add the water, orange juice, juice from 1 lime, bay leaves, and garlic.

4 Close the lid and the steam valve. Set the cooker to high pressure for 120 minutes. Let the cooker release pressure naturally for 15 minutes before releasing the rest of the pressure manually.

5 Remove the pork from the pot and shred it. If you don't plan on using it right away, store it with a cup or two (235 to 475 ml) of the pot juices to keep it moist.

6 When you're ready to eat it, preheat the oven to 425°F (220°C, or gas mark 7). Put the remaining ¼ cup (60 ml) of bacon drippings in a large rimmed baking sheet and put it in the oven until it gets hot, but not smoking.

7 Break the pork into bite-size pieces. Pull the pan out of the oven and immediately spread the pork on the pan. Return the pan to the oven and roast for 10-15 minutes, tossing the pork around with a pair of tongs, until it is mostly golden brown with crispy edges. Taste and sprinkle some salt over the pork, if necessary. Squeeze the juice from the remaining lime over the pork.

8 Transfer the pork to a serving dish and serve with desired fixings.

Smoky Orange Molasses Ribs

Every time I develop a pork recipe, I'm drawn to fruit. Fruit pairs so well with pork! This time I went with oranges and made a dark, sticky sauce that will stick to your fingers and your face. It's well worth the extra napkins.

Prep time 15 minutes
Pressure time 18 minutes + 10 minutes natural release + 5-7 minutes broiling time
Serves 6

1 full rack of baby back pork ribs
2 teaspoons sea salt
1 teaspoon zest and the juice of 1 large orange, divided
1 tablespoon (9 g) coconut sugar
1 teaspoon chili powder
1 teaspoon ground coriander

Pinch of crushed red pepper flakes
¼ cup (80 g) molasses
2 tablespoons (28 ml) balsamic vinegar
½ teaspoon liquid smoke (optional)
¼ cup (60 ml) chicken broth, homemade (page 242) or store-bought

1 Cut the rack of ribs in half and place them on a sheet pan or a large platter that will prevent liquid from running off onto the counter.

2 In a small bowl, combine the salt, orange zest, coconut sugar, chili powder, coriander, and red pepper flakes. Rub the mixture all over the ribs.

3 Combine the molasses, vinegar, and liquid smoke and drizzle the mixture over the meaty part of the ribs.

4 Prepare your cooker by placing the wire rack inside the pot and pouring in the orange juice and the chicken broth. Place the ribs in the pot, standing on end and leaning against the sides of the pot. Pour any juices from the seasoning mixture remaining on the sheet pan over the ribs as well.

5 Close the lid and the steam valve and set the cooker to high pressure for 18 minutes. Let the pressure release naturally for 10 minutes and then release the rest manually.

6 Meanwhile, line a clean rimmed baking sheet with aluminum foil and turn your oven to high broil.

7 When the ribs are finished, place them on the prepared baking sheet, meaty-side up. (Save the cooking juices.) Broil on an upper oven rack for 5-7 minutes until the ribs are golden brown. Brush them with the cooking juices once or twice toward the end of broiling.

8 Slice the ribs into 1- or 2-rib portions and serve with the cooking juices.

Note: The liquid smoke gives the ribs a more pronounced smoky flavor. You can find it near the BBQ sauces or in the spice section in most grocery stores.

Honey Mustard Ribs

This tangy, lightly sweetened take on ribs is a fun change from traditional BBQ ribs. I'm always amazed at how quickly a pressure cooker can tenderize a full rack of ribs. If your ribs don't pull away easily from the bone when you take them out, pressurize them again for a few more minutes. Finishing them under the broiler (or on the grill if you like!) caramelizes the tops and adds even more flavor.

Prep time 15 minutes
Pressure time 18 minutes + 10 minutes natural release + 5-7 minutes broiling time
Serves 6

1 full rack of baby back pork ribs
2 teaspoons sea salt
1 teaspoon black pepper
¼ cup (60 g) Dijon mustard
2 tablespoons (40 g) honey
1 tablespoon (15 ml) coconut aminos

1 tablespoon (15 ml) apple cider vinegar
1 tablespoon (9 g) coconut sugar
½ teaspoon dried thyme
½ teaspoon onion powder
½ cup (120 ml) chicken broth, homemade (page 242) or store-bought

1 Cut the rack of ribs in half and place them on a sheet pan or a large platter that will prevent liquid from running off onto the counter.

2 Sprinkle both sides with the salt and pepper.

3 In a small bowl, combine the mustard, honey, coconut aminos, vinegar, coconut sugar, thyme, and onion powder. Pour half of the mixture over the ribs, turning the ribs to coat both sides. Reserve the other half for basting later.

4 Prepare your cooker by placing the wire rack inside the pot and pouring in the chicken broth. Place the ribs in the pot, standing on end and leaning against the sides of the pot. Pour any juices from the seasoning mixture remaining on the sheet pan over the ribs as well.

5 Close the lid and the steam valve and set the cooker to high pressure for 18 minutes. Let the pressure release naturally for 10 minutes and then release the rest manually.

6 Meanwhile, line a clean rimmed baking sheet with aluminum foil and turn your oven to high broil.

7 When the ribs are finished, place them on the prepared baking sheet, meaty-side up. (Leave the cooking juices in the pot.)

8 Pour the reserved honey-Dijon mixture into the pot with the cooking juices. Turn the cooker to the high sauté mode and whisk. Let it simmer for a few minutes to thicken slightly.

9 Place the pan with the ribs on an upper rack for 5-7 minutes until the ribs are golden brown. Brush the ribs a couple of times with the cooking juices toward the end of cooking.

10 Slice the ribs into 1- or 2-rib portions and serve with a drizzle of cooking juices.

Moroccan-Spiced Ribs with Garlic Sauce

There's a recipe on my website for grilled Moroccan chicken using a simple spice and herb blend. That blend works equally well on ribs! Don't forget the garlic sauce— it's what brings the whole recipe together.

Prep time 15 minutes

Pressure time 18 minutes + 10 minutes natural release + 5-7 minutes broiling time

Serves 6

1 full rack of pork baby back ribs

2 teaspoons sea salt

1 teaspoon black pepper

1 tablespoon (10 g) minced garlic

4 teaspoons (10 g) ground cumin

4 teaspoons (10 g) paprika

¼ teaspoon crushed red pepper flakes

⅛ teaspoon ground cinnamon

3 tablespoons (9 g) chopped chives or (18 g) thinly sliced scallion

½ cup (120 ml) chicken broth, homemade (page 242) or store-bought

For the garlic sauce:

4 cloves of garlic

Pinch of sea salt

3 tablespoons (42 g) Paleo-Friendly Mayonnaise (page 230)

⅓ cup (80 ml) olive oil

1 Cut the rack of ribs in half and place them on a sheet pan or a large platter that will prevent liquid from running off onto the counter.

2 Sprinkle both sides with the salt and pepper.

3 In a small bowl, mix the garlic, cumin, paprika, red pepper flakes, and cinnamon. Rub the mixture all over the ribs and sprinkle the chives over the ribs, too.

4 Prepare your cooker by placing the wire rack inside the pot and pouring in the chicken broth. Place the ribs in the pot, standing on end and leaning against the sides of the pot.

5 Close the lid and the steam valve and set the cooker to high pressure for 18 minutes. Let the pressure release naturally for 10 minutes and then release the rest manually.

6 Meanwhile, line a clean rimmed baking sheet with aluminum foil and turn your oven to high broil.

7 To make the garlic sauce, chop the garlic and then sprinkle it with salt and smash it all together with the side of your knife to form a paste. Transfer it to a small bowl and mix in the Paleo-Friendly Mayonnaise. While whisking, slowly drizzle in the olive oil to form an emulsion. Cover and chill until ready to use.

8 When the ribs are finished, place them on the prepared baking sheet, meaty-side up. (Save the cooking juices.) Broil on an upper oven rack for 5-7 minutes until the outsides have crisped up a bit.

9 Slice the ribs and serve with the garlic sauce.

Teriyaki-Glazed Pork Roast

This Asian-style pork roast was a favorite among my recipe testers! After the roast spends time in the pressure cooker, it's finished in the oven with a sticky, sweet-savory glaze. The leftovers also make quick and tasty lunches throughout the week.

Prep time 10 minutes

Pressure time 20 minutes +
15 minutes natural release + 10–15 minutes roasting time + 10 minutes resting time

Serves 8

One 3-pound (1.4 kg) pork loin or sirloin roast (not tenderloin)

1 cup (235 ml) chicken broth, homemade (page 242) or store-bought

2 tablespoons (16 g) finely grated ginger

1 tablespoon (10 g) minced garlic

1 tablespoon (15 ml) coconut aminos

1 tablespoon (15 ml) fish sauce

1 tablespoon (15 ml) rice vinegar

1 teaspoon sea salt

1 teaspoon Asian chili garlic sauce

½ cup (120 ml) Paleo Teriyaki Sauce (page 236), divided

1 Score the top of the roast with 3–4 slices, ½–1 inch (1.3–2.5 cm) deep. If your roast has a fatty side, make the slits there.

2 Put the chicken broth in the pot with the wire rack and place the roast on the rack.

3 Combine the ginger, garlic, coconut aminos, fish sauce, rice vinegar, salt, and Asian chili garlic sauce in a small bowl. Pour the mixture over the roast, getting it inside the slits on the top.

4 Close the lid and the steam valve. Set the cooker to high pressure for 20 minutes.

5 Preheat your oven to 450°F (230°C, or gas mark 8).

6 Let the pressure release naturally for 15 minutes and then release the rest of the pressure manually.

7 Transfer the roast to a foil-lined baking dish or baking pan. Put it in the oven and roast for 10–15 minutes to finish cooking and develop a golden brown crust. Brush the outside with ¼ cup (60 ml) of the Paleo Teriyaki Sauce two or three times during the last few minutes. The center of the roast should read 145°F (63°C) with an instant-read thermometer.

8 While the roast is in the oven, remove the wire rack from the cooker and turn on the high sauté mode. Add the remaining ¼ cup (60 ml) of Paleo Teriyaki Sauce to the pot and simmer for 10 minutes to reduce it and thicken it up a bit. You should have 1½–2 cups (355–475 ml) of sauce in the pot.

9 Remove the roast from the oven and let it rest for 10 minutes before slicing.

10 Serve the pork with the sauce from the pot.

Italian Sausage Meatballs and Marinara

Using Italian sausage in meatballs gives them a giant boost of flavor! If you have trouble finding clean bulk Italian sausage, you can substitute plain ground pork and increase the amount of Italian seasoning by 1 teaspoon and add an extra clove of garlic.

Prep time 15 minutes

Pressure time 5 minutes + 5 minutes natural release

Serves 6

1 pound (455 g) bulk Italian sausage (pork or chicken)

1 pound (455 g) ground turkey

1½ teaspoons sea salt

2 teaspoons Italian seasoning

1 tablespoon (15 ml) coconut aminos

1 tablespoon (4 g) nutritional yeast, plus more for serving

2 egg whites

1 tablespoon (7 g) coconut flour

4 cloves of garlic, minced

Spiralized vegetable noodles (butternut squash, sweet potato, or zucchini)

4 tablespoons (60 ml) avocado oil, divided

One 36-ounce (1 kg) jar marinara sauce

Scallions, thinly sliced, for garnish

1 Combine the sausage, ground turkey, salt, Italian seasoning, coconut aminos, nutritional yeast, egg whites, coconut flour, and garlic in a large mixing bowl. Use your hands to gently blend the mixture until everything is mixed well.

2 If you plan on boiling your squash noodles, now would be a good time to start a pot of water to boil.

3 Roll the meat mixture into 2-inch (5 cm) meatballs and place them on a large plate.

4 Add 2 tablespoons (28 ml) of the avocado oil to the cooker insert and turn it to high sauté. When the pot has preheated, add half of the meatballs to the skillet and let them cook, undisturbed, for 3-4 minutes until a brown crust forms on the bottoms and they release easily from the pan. Turn them and brown the other sides. They do not need to be cooked all the way through at this point. Transfer them back to the plate and brown the second batch of meatballs in the remaining 2 tablespoons (28 ml) of avocado oil.

When those are finished browning, return the other meatballs back to the pot and turn off the cooker.

5 Pour the marinara sauce over the meatballs. Set the cooker to high pressure for 5 minutes. Let the cooker release pressure naturally for 5 minutes before releasing the pressure manually.

6 Cook the spiralized squash either in that pot of boiling water for 2-5 minutes, depending on the thickness of the noodles, or in a separate skillet over medium-high heat with a drizzle of avocado oil and a sprinkling of salt and pepper, tossing often, for 4-6 minutes.

7 Check the sauce when the meatballs are done. If it is too watery, remove the meatballs to a serving dish and cover to keep warm. Turn the cooker to the high sauté mode and cook for several minutes until the sauce is reduced some.

8 Serve the meatballs and sauce over a bed of vegetable noodles and top with a sprinkling of sliced scallions and nutritional yeast.

Mustard-Herb Pork Roast with Maple-Butternut Mash

This juicy pork roast and sweet butternut mash works well for a weeknight meal, but is also fancy enough for a special occasion or a small group of friends for the holidays. Using precut butternut squash makes this an even quicker meal to prep.

Prep time 15 minutes +
2 hours marinating time

Pressure time 18 minutes +
15 minutes natural release + 10–15 minutes
roasting + 10 minutes resting time

Serves 8

One 3-pound (1.4 kg) pork loin roast

2 tablespoons (30 g) Dijon mustard

1 tablespoon (15 g) sea salt

3 tablespoons (45 ml) avocado
oil, divided

1 teaspoon dried crushed rosemary

1 teaspoon dried rubbed sage or
¼ teaspoon ground sage

½ teaspoon black pepper

¼ cup (60 ml) chicken broth,
homemade (page 242) or store-bought

2 pounds (900 g) cubed
butternut squash

2 shallots, thinly sliced

¼ cup (60 ml) pure maple syrup

1 Place the pork roast on a large platter or small baking sheet. Combine the mustard, salt, 1 tablespoon (15 ml) of the avocado oil, rosemary, sage, and pepper in a small bowl. Stir to create a paste and then rub the paste over the entire pork roast. Cover the roast with plastic wrap and chill for at least 2 hours, up to 12 hours.

2 When you're ready to cook the roast, turn your cooker to the high sauté setting and add the remaining 2 tablespoons (28 ml) of avocado oil to the pot.

3 Place the roast, fat-side down, in the pot and sear for 3–4 minutes. Flip the roast over and sear the other side for 3–4 minutes. Transfer the roast to a large plate and add the chicken broth to the pot. Scrape up any bits that have stuck to the pot and then turn the cooker off.

4 Add the squash and shallots to the pot, sprinkle with a pinch of salt and pepper, and then put the wire rack on top. Place the roast, fat-side up, on the wire rack. Pour the maple syrup over the roast.

5 Close the lid and the steam valve. Set the cooker to high pressure for 18 minutes.

6 Preheat your oven to 450°F (230°C, or gas mark 8) and line a baking pan (that will fit the roast) with aluminum foil.

Note: If you happen to have any pork leftover, chop it up and add it to your breakfast hashes or rice dishes throughout the week. Leftover butternut mash can be frozen and reheated later to thicken chili or any other hearty soup. Side note: I know from personal experience that babies love that butternut mash. If you have a little one at home, you can freeze leftovers in an ice cube tray for easy meals later on!

7 When the roast is done, let the pressure release naturally for 15 minutes before releasing the rest manually.

8 Transfer the roast to the foil-lined baking dish and roast it in the oven for 10–15 minutes to finish cooking and develop a golden brown crust. If it starts to get dark too quickly, tent the roast with a piece of foil. The center should read 145°F (63°C) with an instant-read thermometer.

9 Meanwhile, transfer the squash with a slotted spoon to a food processor, leaving any juices in the pan. Blend the squash until smooth, adding some pot juices, if necessary, to reach the desired consistency. If you don't have a food processor, mash the squash with a potato masher in a medium bowl. Taste and add a little salt if necessary.

10 Let the pork rest for 10 minutes before slicing. Slice the pork and serve it with the butternut squash mash and a drizzle of pan juices.

Garlic-Lime Pork Roast with Strawberry-Mango Salsa

To be honest, I was never a fan of pork roast until recently. The first time I had a pork roast I loved was at a conference I attended several years ago, and it totally changed the way I viewed pork roast. The meat was juicier and more flavorful than any pork roast I had tried in the past. The most memorable part was the mango salsa that was served alongside. I created my own version of that pork roast with its sweet, fruity salsa.

Prep time 20 minutes

Pressure time 18 minutes + 10 minutes natural release + 10-15 minutes roasting time + 5 minutes resting time

Serves 8

For the salsa:

1 pound (455 g) vine or Roma tomatoes, diced

2 cups (340 g) chopped strawberries

1 ripe mango, peeled, pitted, and diced

1 jalapeño, seeded (optional) and diced

½ cup (80 g) diced red onion

⅓ cup (5 g) chopped fresh cilantro

1 lime

Pinch of sea salt

For the pork:

1 cup (235 ml) chicken broth, homemade (page 242) or store-bought

One 3-pound (1.4 kg) pork loin roast

1 tablespoon (15 g) sea salt

¼ teaspoon black pepper

⅛ teaspoon crushed red pepper flakes

6 cloves of garlic, smashed

Zest and juice of 2 limes

1 tablespoon (8 g) tapioca flour

¼ cup (60 ml) water

1 To make the salsa, combine the tomatoes, strawberries, mango, jalapeño, onion, and cilantro in a medium bowl. Add the juice from ½ of the lime and a generous pinch of salt. Reserve the other ½ lime for later. Chill the salsa until ready to serve.

2 To make the pork, put the chicken broth and the wire rack in the bottom of the the pressure cooker pot.

3 Place the pork roast on a cutting board or other flat surface. Cut six 1-inch (2.5 cm)-deep slits in the fatty side of the roast. Sprinkle the salt, pepper, and red pepper flakes all over the roast. Insert a smashed garlic clove into each slit.

4 Combine the lime zest and juice in a small bowl. Pour the mixture over the roast, getting it into the slits as well.

5 Close the lid and the steam valve. Set the cooker to high pressure for 20 minutes. Let the pressure release naturally for 15 minutes before releasing the rest manually.

6 Meanwhile, preheat your oven to 450°F (230°C, or gas mark 8). Line a baking sheet with foil.

7 Transfer the roast to the prepared baking sheet and finish cooking it in the oven to form a golden crust on the outside and bring the interior temperature to 145°F (63°C). This should take 10-15 minutes.

8 Meanwhile, turn your cooker to high sauté. Whisk the tapioca flour into the water and slowly drizzle it into the pot juices while whisking. The sauce should thicken up in a minute or so. Turn the cooker off.

9 Brush the roast with the sauce a couple of times toward the end of roasting. When it is finished, take it out of the oven and tent it with foil to keep it warm and allow it to rest for 5 minutes before slicing.

10 Slice the roast, squirt the juice from the reserved ½ lime over the top, and serve it with the sauce from the pot and the salsa.

Pork and Cabbage Egg Roll Bowls

Even if I weren't avoiding fried food, I think I'd prefer these egg roll bowls over homemade fried egg rolls. They're much easier to make, and there isn't an epic grease splatter mess to clean up afterward. These bowls whip up quickly and are perfect for a weeknight meal.

Prep time 20 minutes
Pressure time 2 minutes
Serves 6

Note: To save time, you can use a couple of 12-ounce (340 g) bags of shredded cabbage.

1 tablespoon (15 ml) sesame oil

1 pound (455 g) ground pork

½ teaspoon Chinese five-spice powder

½ teaspoon sea salt

1 large shallot, chopped (or ½ medium onion, diced)

1 bell pepper (any color), seeded and diced

2 large carrots, peeled and diced

3 tablespoons (45 ml) coconut aminos

1 tablespoon (15 ml) fish sauce

1 tablespoon (8 g) finely grated ginger

2 teaspoons minced garlic

Pinch of crushed red pepper flakes (optional, if you'd like to add a little heat)

¼ cup (60 ml) chicken broth, homemade (page 242) or store-bought

1 medium head of green cabbage, trimmed and chopped

Roasted Cauliflower Rice (page 200) or hot jasmine rice, for serving

4 scallions, thinly sliced, for serving

Asian chili garlic paste, for serving

1 Turn the cooker to high sauté and add the sesame oil to the pot. When the pot has preheated, add the ground pork. Break up the pork into small bits as it cooks and cook until the pork gets golden brown and begins to stick to the pot somewhat, 8–12 minutes.

2 Add the five-spice powder, salt, and shallot. Cook for another couple of minutes until the shallots begin to soften.

3 Add the bell pepper, carrots, coconut aminos, fish sauce, ginger, garlic, red pepper flakes (if using), and chicken broth. Stir well, scraping up any bits that have stuck (but not scorched) to the bottom of the pot. Add the cabbage.

4 Close the lid and the steam valve. Set the cooker to high pressure for 2 minutes. Use a manual quick release to release the pressure.

5 Stir the mixture. If there is too much liquid to your liking, then set the cooker to high sauté for a few minutes to let some of that cook off.

6 Serve with cauliflower or jasmine rice with a sprinkle of scallions and some Asian chili garlic paste.

Pork and Apple Stew

Pork and apples is a classic flavor combination, and I brought the two together with a creamy gravy in a stew. This is healthy comfort food at its finest.

Prep time 20 minutes

Pressure time 10 minutes + 5 minutes natural release

Serves 6

2 tablespoons (28 ml) ghee (page 234) or avocado oil, divided

1 pound (455 g) boneless pork loin or chops, cut into 1-inch (2.5 cm) pieces

1½ teaspoons sea salt, divided

¼ teaspoon black pepper

1 pound (455 g) red potatoes, cut into 1-inch (2.5 cm) pieces

2 medium tart apples, peeled and cut into 1-inch (2.5 cm) pieces

2 large carrots, peeled and cut into ½-inch (1.3 cm) pieces

1 cup (160 g) diced sweet onion

1 cup (235 ml) chicken broth, homemade (page 242) or store-bought, divided

2 tablespoons (28 ml) apple cider vinegar

2 tablespoons (30 g) whole-grain mustard

1 teaspoon minced garlic

1 tablespoon (8 g) tapioca or (9 g) arrowroot flour

1 Turn on the cooker to the high sauté setting. Add 1 tablespoon (15 ml) of the avocado oil to the pot.

2 Sprinkle the pork with ½ teaspoon of the salt and the pepper. Add half of the pork to the pot and cook for 3-4 minutes, flipping it around once or twice, until some golden brown spots form. Remove the pork and add the remaining 1 tablespoon (15 ml) of avocado oil and the other half of the pork. Cook for 3-4 minutes as well. Add the rest of the pork to the pot and turn off the cooker.

3 Add the potatoes, apples, carrots, onion, and remaining teaspoon of salt.

4 Whisk together ¾ cup (175 ml) of the chicken broth, vinegar, mustard, and garlic. Pour it into the pot and give it a good stir.

5 Close the lid and the steam valve. Set the cooker to high pressure for 10 minutes. Let the cooker release pressure naturally for 5 minutes and then release the rest manually.

6 Whisk together the remaining ¼ cup (60 ml) of chicken broth and the tapioca flour. Pour it into the pot and stir it for a minute or so. The residual heat from the pot should be enough to thicken the sauce, but if it isn't thickening, then turn the pot to sauté for a minute or two. As you stir, the apples will break down and help make the sauce creamy.

7 Serve the stew alone or with a side dish of your choice.

Quick and Easy Kielbasa and Sauerkraut Sweet Potato Mash

If you need a lightning-fast yet hearty weeknight meal, this is it. It's getting easier to find clean, grass-fed sausages these days, too. Kielbasa is one of my favorites—I love its peppery bite with a touch of heat.

Prep time 10 minutes
Pressure time 5 minutes
Serves 4

2½–3 pounds (1.1–1.4 kg) sweet potatoes, cut into 1-inch (2.5 cm) pieces

1 teaspoon sea salt

1 cup (142 g) drained sauerkraut + ½ cup (120 ml) juice from the jar, divided

4 large kielbasa links (about 12 ounces [340 g])

1–2 tablespoons (15–28 ml) ghee (page 234) or (14 to 28 g) grass-fed butter

Whole-grain mustard, for serving

1 Pour 1 cup (235 ml) of water into the pot and place a steam basket inside.

2 Put the sweet potatoes in the steam basket and sprinkle the salt over top. Add the sauerkraut on top of the sweet potatoes and the kielbasa links on top.

3 Close the lid and the steam valve. Set the cooker to high pressure for 5 minutes. When the cycle is finished, manually release all of the pressure.

4 Transfer the kielbasa and most of the sauerkraut to a plate. Transfer the potatoes to a large bowl. Add the sauerkraut juice, ghee, and salt. Mash thoroughly. Add more juice, if necessary. Taste and adjust the salt, if needed.

5 Serve the kielbasa, sauerkraut, and sweet potato mash with some whole-grain mustard.

Cashew Pork with Bok Choy

Bok choy tends to fly under the radar for me, but when I use it, I wonder why I don't use it more often. It's a sturdy cruciferous vegetable, mild in flavor, and works well in quick, high-heat cooking. Bok choy is widely available, but if you have trouble finding it, you can substitute a half head of green cabbage.

Prep time 15 minutes
Pressure time 5 minutes + 5 minutes natural release
Serves 6

½ teaspoon sea salt

1 pound (455 g) pork loin, cut into 1-inch (2.5 cm) pieces

2 tablespoons (28 ml) sesame oil, divided

2 teaspoons minced garlic

2 teaspoons minced or grated ginger

1 cup (160 g) chopped sweet onion

1 cup (140 g) whole, raw cashews

2 heads of bok choy, quartered and chopped (2½–3 cups [175–210 g])

¼ cup (60 ml) coconut aminos

1 tablespoon (15 ml) mirin or rice vinegar

1½ teaspoons fish sauce

Pinch of crushed red pepper flakes

1 cup (235 ml) chicken broth, homemade (page 242) or store-bought, divided

1 tablespoon (8 g) tapioca or (9 g) arrowroot flour

Roasted Cauliflower Rice (page 200), for serving

Asian chili garlic sauce for serving

1 Sprinkle the salt on the cubed pork.

2 Turn the cooker on the high sauté setting and add 1 tablespoon (15 ml) of the sesame oil to the pot. When it has preheated, add half of the pork to the pot and cook until a golden crust forms. Flip them around and cook for another few minutes until browned on the other side. Remove the pork from the pot and repeat with the remaining 1 tablespoon (15 ml) of sesame oil and the rest of the pork. When that batch is finished, return all of the pork to the cooker and turn it off.

3 Add the garlic, ginger, onion, cashews, bok choy, coconut aminos, mirin, fish sauce, red pepper flakes, and ½ cup (120 ml) of the chicken broth to the pot. Give it a good stir.

4 Close the lid and the steam valve. Set the cooker to high pressure for 5 minutes. Let the cooker release the pressure naturally for 5 minutes and then release the rest of the pressure manually.

5 Whisk together the remaining ½ cup (120 ml) of chicken broth with the tapioca flour. Open the lid to the cooker and slowly pour in the chicken broth mixture while stirring the cashew pork around. Set the cooker to medium sauté and simmer for a minute or two until the sauce has thickened.

6 Serve with the Roasted Cauliflower Rice and a little Asian chili garlic sauce if you like some heat.

Sausage and Sweet Potato Make-Ahead Scramble Cups

If you're a fan of prepping meals ahead of time, this is the perfect recipe for you. After you make a batch of these scramble cups, just store them in the fridge and empty one into a skillet for a quick, tasty breakfast scramble. Feel free to play with the vegetables and seasonings and make them your own. You'll need seven half-pint (235 ml) mason jars (the tall, regular-mouth ones all fit in a 6-quart [5.7 L] cooker without stacking).

Prep time 20 minutes

Pressure time 10 minutes + 2 minutes natural release

Makes 7 half-pint (235 ml) jars

8 ounces (225 g) bulk breakfast sausage or precooked sausage, diced

1 tablespoon (15 ml) avocado oil (optional, if using precooked sausage)

8 eggs

1½ teaspoons sea salt

1 cup (235 ml) almond or coconut milk

1½ teaspoon smoked paprika

2 teaspoons minced garlic

1 small sweet potato, spiralized or diced into ½-inch (1.3 cm) cubes (about 2 cups [266 g])

1½ cups (225 g) chopped cherry or grape tomatoes

1½ cups (45 g) chopped baby spinach

Salsa, hot sauce, and guacamole, for serving (optional)

1 Cook the breakfast sausage in a skillet over medium-high heat until it is fully cooked and has crispy bits throughout. If you're using pre-cooked sausage, just toast it in the pan with the avocado oil until golden brown. Remove from the heat and set aside.

2 Meanwhile, whisk together the eggs, salt, milk, paprika, and garlic in a medium bowl or large glass measuring cup (makes it easier for pouring later).

3 Divide the sausage, sweet potato cubes, tomatoes, and spinach among the mason jars. Then, divide the egg mixture among the jars, filling them about two-thirds full.

4 Put the wire rack and 1 cup (235 ml) of water in your pot. Arrange the mason jars on the wire rack.

5 Close the lid and the steam valve. Set the cooker to high pressure for 10 minutes. Let the pressure release naturally for 2 minutes and then release the rest of the pressure manually.

6 Carefully remove the jars from the pot and let cool until you can handle them safely.

7 Serve the omelet cups with salsa, hot sauce, and guacamole, if desired.

VEGETABLE SIDES

Whipping up a quick batch of mashed potatoes or cooking a spaghetti squash is a great way to get over any initial intimidation when you first start using your multicooker. Vegetable sides might often be afterthoughts, but they certainly don't have to be boring. Recipes like Bacon-Ranch Potato Salad (page 188) and Spaghetti Squash with Sun-Dried Pesto (page 195) might even upstage the main offering.

Recipes

German Sweet and Sour Cabbage (Rotkohl)

I have a soft spot for German and Austrian food after spending a year and a half there during my college years. Rotkohl is a staple in German cuisine and is often served alongside breaded pork cutlets and potatoes like my Hot German Potato Salad with Sauerkraut and Bacon (page 190). It also pairs well with grilled meats.

Prep time 15 minutes

Pressure time 3 minutes + 5 minutes natural release

Serves 8–10

2 tablespoons (28 ml) bacon drippings or ghee (page 234)

1 large onion, thinly sliced

2 large tart apples, peeled, cored, halved, and thinly sliced

1 cup (235 ml) red wine vinegar

5 tablespoons (75 g) Date Paste (page 232) or (100 g) honey

1 large head of red cabbage, thinly sliced or shredded

1 teaspoon sea salt

2 bay leaves

Pinch of ground cloves

¼ cup (60 ml) vegetable or chicken broth, homemade (page 242) or store-bought

1 Turn the cooker to the high sauté setting. Add your fat of choice to the pot and when it has preheated, add the onions. Cook, stirring occasionally, until the onions have softened.

2 Add the apples, vinegar, and sweetener. Stir to incorporate the sweetener. Add the cabbage. Place the lid on the pot, but do not seal. Let it steam the cabbage, tossing the cabbage around with tongs a few times until it has wilted down a couple of inches (5 cm), about 5 minutes.

3 Add the salt, bay leaves, cloves, and broth.

4 Close the lid and the steam valve. Set the cooker to high pressure for 3 minutes. Let the cooker release the pressure naturally for at least 5 minutes and then manually release the rest of the pressure.

5 Open the lid, remove the bay leaves, and stir the cabbage around—especially if you used date paste and you can still see clumps of it. A quick stir will blend it nicely.

6 You can serve this anytime, but I prefer it after it has cooled for a while or even the next day.

Note: You can certainly use coconut or avocado oil in this, but I love the extra boost of flavor the bacon drippings give.

Colcannon

It surprises me how a recipe with such simple, peasant-type ingredients can turn out so delicious. If you're planning an Irish-themed or St. Patrick's Day dinner, this is a must-have. It goes really well with my Home-Brined Corned Beef and Cabbage (page 118), too!

Prep time: 15 minutes

Pressure time: 5 minutes + 5-10 minutes natural release

Serves 6

4 tablespoons (60 ml) ghee (page 234) or (112 g) grass-fed butter, divided

1 small head of green cabbage, shredded

2½ pounds (1.1 kg) red potatoes, cut into 1-inch (2.5 cm) cubes

¼ cup (60 ml) chicken broth, homemade (page 242) or store-bought

1½ teaspoons sea salt

¼ cup (60 ml) almond or coconut milk

4 scallions, trimmed and thinly sliced

1 Set the cooker to the high sauté setting. Add 2 tablespoons (28 ml) of the ghee to the pot. When the pot has preheated, add the cabbage. Sauté, using tongs to stir it around, until the cabbage is tender, has reduced by at least half, and looks translucent.

2 Add the potatoes, chicken broth, and salt.

3 Close the lid and the steam valve. Set the cooker to high pressure for 5 minutes. Allow the pressure to reduce naturally for 5-10 minutes and then release the rest manually, if you like.

4 Remove the lid and add the almond milk. Mash the potatoes and the cabbage with a potato masher and then stir in the scallions. Taste and add more salt and the remaining 2 tablespoons (28 ml) of ghee, if needed.

Whole Steamed Potatoes

Steaming potatoes in a pressure cooker frees up space in your oven or stovetop for other things during meal preparation and creates the creamiest "baked" potatoes!

Prep time: 5 minutes

Pressure time: 15 minutes + 10 minutes natural release

Makes 5-6 potatoes

5-6 whole white or sweet potatoes, 6-9 ounces (170-255 g) each

1 Put 1 cup (235 ml) of water and the wire rack into the pot.

2 Poke the potatoes a few times with a sharp knife and place them on the wire rack.

3 Close the lid and the steam valve and set the cooker to high pressure for 15 minutes. If the potatoes are a little smaller, reduce the time by 2 minutes. If they're a little bigger, increase by 2 minutes.

4 Let the cooker release pressure on its own for 10 minutes and then release the rest of the pressure manually. Leave the potatoes in the cooker to keep warm until serving.

Steakhouse Mashed Potatoes

I love the hearty, chunky mashed potatoes that are commonly served at a steak-house restaurant. Peeling the potatoes is optional, but the ghee or butter really isn't.

Prep time 10 minutes
Pressure time 15 minutes
Serves 6

4 pounds (1.8 kg) Yukon gold or red potatoes, cut into 2-inch (5 cm) chunks (peeling optional)

½ cup (120 ml) ghee (page 234) or (112 g) grass-fed butter

½ –1 cup (120–235 ml) unsweetened almond milk

2 teaspoons minced garlic

2 teaspoons sea salt

½ teaspoon coarsely ground black pepper

1 Put 1 cup (235 ml) of water and the wire rack into the pot. Place a steam basket on the wire rack.

2 Put the potatoes in the steam basket. Close the lid and the steam valve. Set the cooker to high pressure for 15 minutes. Use a quick release to let out the pressure.

3 Meanwhile, put the ghee, milk, and garlic in a small saucepan. Heat until everything is melted and combined. Remove from the heat and let it sit until the potatoes are finished.

4 Transfer the potatoes to a large bowl and mash them a little. Pour the warm milk mixture into the bowl, add the salt and pepper, and continue to mash the potatoes until you reach your preferred texture. Taste and add more salt, if needed.

5 Serve warm.

Chile-Orange Mashed Sweet Potatoes

This might seem like an odd flavor combination, but trust me. Sweet potatoes and oranges pair so well together and the heat from the chile breaks up the sweetness. It's a perfect trifecta. These mashed sweet potatoes would be delicious with some grilled steaks or pork chops.

Prep time 15 minutes
Pressure time 15 minutes
Serves 6

½ cup (120 ml) ghee (page 234) or (112 g) grass-fed butter

Zest from ½ orange

⅛ teaspoon crushed red pepper flakes

2 tablespoons (28 ml) apple cider vinegar

3–3½ pounds (1.4–1.6 kg) sweet potatoes, peeled and cut into 2-inch (5 cm) chunks

1 teaspoon sea salt

1 In a small saucepan or skillet, combine the ghee, orange zest, and red pepper flakes and heat until it's steamy, but don't boil it. Remove from the heat and add the vinegar. Let the mixture sit until ready to use.

2 Put 1 cup (235 ml) of water and the wire rack into the pressure cooker pot. Place the steam basket on the wire rack.

3 Put the potatoes in the steam basket. Close the lid and the steam valve. Set the cooker to high pressure for 15 minutes. Use a quick release to let out the pressure.

4 Transfer the potatoes to a large bowl and pour the ghee mixture over them. Add the salt. Mash until the desired consistency is reached. Taste and add more salt, if needed.

5 Serve warm.

Russian Beet and Potato Salad

This recipe is somewhat sentimental. My husband and I met in Russia almost twenty years ago and ate a lot of salads similar to this. Beets and potatoes are a staple in Russian cuisine, and I love how they pair them with briny pickles and fresh dill.

Prep time 20 minutes
Pressure time 10 minutes + 5 minutes natural release
Serves 6

1 pound (455 g) small beets, trimmed and peeled

1½ pounds (680 g) medium red or Yukon gold potatoes

1 cup (143 g) chopped dill pickles

⅓ cup (37 g) minced carrot

2½ – 3 cups (338–405 g) diced English cucumber (about 1 large)

3 scallions, thinly sliced

⅔ cup (43 g) chopped fresh dill or 2 teaspoons dried dill

⅓ cup (20 g) chopped fresh parsley

½ cup (115 g) Paleo-Friendly Mayonnaise (page 230)

¼ cup (60 ml) pickle juice (from the jar)

2 tablespoons (28 ml) red wine vinegar

1½ teaspoons sea salt

1 Your beets should be half the size of your potatoes. Halve the large beets, if needed, so they cook evenly. Put ½ cup (120 ml) of water and the wire rack into the pot. Place the steam basket on the wire rack.

2 Place the beets and potatoes in the steam basket. Close the lid and the steam valve and set the cooker to high pressure for 10 minutes. Let the cooker release pressure for 5 minutes on its own and then release the rest of the pressure manually.

3 While the vegetables are cooking, prep the pickles, carrots, cucumbers, scallions, dill, and parsley. Put them in a large mixing bowl.

4 Whisk together the Paleo-Friendly Mayonnaise, pickle juice, vinegar, and salt in a small bowl. Set aside.

5 When the potatoes and beets are finished, transfer them to a cutting board and let them cool for a few minutes. Chop the potatoes and beets into ½ -inch (1.3 cm) cubes and place them in the bowl with the vegetables. Pour the dressing over the top and gently fold everything together until mixed well.

6 Serve warm or cold.

Bacon-Ranch Potato Salad

It may seem overly confident of me to say this, but . . . this will be the only potato salad you ever make.

Prep time 15 minutes
Pressure time 5 minutes
Serves 8

4 pounds (1.8 kg) white potatoes, cut into 1-inch (2.5 cm) pieces (peeling optional)

6 eggs

⅔ cup (160 ml) Paleo-Friendly Ranch Dressing (page 237)

½ cup (115 g) Paleo-Friendly Mayonnaise (page 230)

1 cup (143 g) chopped pickles

¼ cup (60 ml) pickle juice (from the jar)

2 tablespoons (22 g) yellow or (30 g) Dijon mustard

1 teaspoon sea salt

¼ teaspoon black pepper

12 slices of cooked, crispy bacon

1 Put 1 cup (235 ml) of water and the wire rack into the pot. Place the steam basket on the wire rack.

2 Place the potatoes in the steam basket and nestle the eggs on the potatoes.

3 Close the lid and the steam valve. Set the cooker to high pressure for 5 minutes. Prepare a medium bowl of ice water to place the eggs in when they come out—this will avoid overcooking them. When the pressure cooking is done, manually release all of the pressure. Immediately remove the eggs and place them into the cold water bath. Leave the potatoes in the open pot to cool for a few minutes.

4 Meanwhile, combine the Paleo-Friendly Ranch Dressing, Paleo-Friendly Mayonnaise, pickles, pickle juice, mustard, salt, and pepper in a small bowl.

5 When the potatoes have cooled enough to handle, transfer them to a large bowl. Peel and dice the eggs; add them to the potatoes. Pour the dressing over the potatoes and eggs and fold everything together gently.

6 Crumble the bacon and sprinkle it on top or fold it into the salad.

Note: An easy way to cook a large batch of bacon is in the oven. You can start it before you prep the potatoes and it'll just about be finished by the time you need it. Just line a rimmed baking sheet with foil and set a wire cooling rack on top. Lay the bacon on the cooling rack close together, but not overlapping. Bake at 400°F (200°C, or gas mark 6) for 25–30 minutes.

Cleanup is easy, too. Just discard (or save!) the bacon drippings and foil. Rinse out the sheet pan and then place the wire rack upside down on the pan and fill it with hot soapy water. Let it sit for a few hours or overnight and it washes off easily.

Hot German Potato Salad with Sauerkraut and Bacon

If you've ever had a hot German potato salad, I urge you to try this version with sauerkraut and bacon! They add a delightful salty-briny flavor to the dish.

Prep time 15 minutes
Pressure time 5 minutes
Serves 8

4 pounds (1.8 kg) white potatoes, cut into 1-inch (2.5 cm) pieces (peeling optional)

8 slices of uncooked, thick-cut bacon, cut into 1-inch (2.5 cm) pieces

½ cup (80 g) small diced sweet onion

½ cup (120 ml) apple cider vinegar

1 tablespoon sweetener ([20 g] honey, [9 g] coconut sugar, or [15 g] Date Paste, page 232)

¼ cup (60 ml) avocado oil

2 teaspoons sea salt

1½ cups (210 g) drained sauerkraut

1 Put 1 cup (235 ml) of water and the wire rack into the pot. Place the steam basket on the wire rack.

2 Place the potatoes in the steam basket. Close the lid and the steam valve. Set the cooker to high pressure for 5 minutes. When the pressure cooking is done, manually release all of the pressure. Leave the potatoes in the open pot to cool for a few minutes.

3 Cook the bacon in a large skillet over medium heat until it reaches the desired crispness, 15–20 minutes. Remove the bacon with a slotted spoon and leave about ⅓ cup (80 ml) of the bacon drippings in the skillet.

4 Return the drippings to medium heat and add the onion. Sauté for 3–4 minutes until the onions are soft and translucent.

5 Whisk in the vinegar, sweetener, avocado oil, and salt. Cook for another minute or so and then remove it from the heat.

6 When the potatoes have cooled enough to handle, transfer them to a large serving bowl. Pour the dressing on top and add the reserved bacon and the sauerkraut. Fold everything together gently. If the potatoes are too hot, they'll mash. (Although making this into a fabulous potato mash wouldn't be a horrible idea.)

Herbed Acorn Squash with Crispy Prosciutto

Have you every toasted prosciutto in a pan? It turns into this crispy, salty chip that makes me think of a cross between potato chips and bacon. I might even like it more than bacon.

Prep time 10 minutes

Pressure time 5 minutes +
10 minutes natural release

Serves 4

1 medium or large acorn squash

¼ teaspoon sea salt

¼ teaspoon ground sage

¼ teaspoon dried thyme

Pinch of crushed red pepper flakes

3 tablespoons (45 ml) melted ghee
(page 234) or (42 g) grass-fed butter

4 slices of prosciutto

1 Cut the squash in half vertically and scrape out the seeds and membranes. Cut the halves in half again.

2 Put 1 cup (235 ml) of water and the rack into the pot and put a steam basket on top.

3 Put the squash quarters, cut-side up, on the rack. Sprinkle the squash with the salt, sage, thyme, and red pepper flakes. Drizzle the ghee over them as well.

4 Close the lid and the steam valve. Set the cooker to high pressure for 5 minutes. Let the cooker release the pressure naturally for 10 minutes and then release the rest of the pressure manually.

5 Meanwhile, cook the prosciutto in a large skillet over medium heat until crispy. Crumble the prosciutto over the squash quarters and serve.

Artichokes with Three Aiolis

My best friend has a traditional pressure cooker that she uses solely for artichokes. I'm pretty sure I've convinced her to use it for other things, but I've got to hand it to her—artichokes are meant to be pressure cooked. Especially if there are three kinds of aioli waiting for them when they come out.

Prep time 10 minutes
Pressure time 8 minutes
Makes 4 large artichokes

4 large artichokes
1 lemon

For the Dijon Aioli:
½ cup (115 g) Paleo-Friendly Mayonnaise (page 230)
2 tablespoons (28 ml) almond or coconut milk
2 teaspoons Dijon mustard
2 teaspoons lemon juice
1 teaspoon minced garlic
Pinch of sea salt

For the Garlic Herb Aioli:
½ cup (115 g) Paleo-Friendly Mayonnaise (page 230)
3 tablespoons (16 g) chopped fresh herbs (dill, parsley, thyme, rosemary)

2 tablespoons (28 ml) almond or coconut milk
2 teaspoons lemon juice
2 teaspoons minced or finely grated garlic
Pinch of sea salt

For the Balsamic Chipotle Bacon Aioli:
½ cup (115 g) Paleo-Friendly Mayonnaise (page 230)
2 tablespoons (28 ml) almond or coconut milk
¼ cup (20 g) minced cooked bacon
4 teaspoons (20 ml) balsamic vinegar
¼ –½ teaspoon chipotle chile powder
Pinch of sea salt

1 Trim any stems from the artichokes and cut off about 1½ inches (3.8 cm) from the top. Squeeze some lemon juice on the cut side so it doesn't turn brown.

2 Put the rack in the bottom of your pot with ½ cup (120 ml) of water. Place the artichokes in there to see if they all fit. At this point, you can choose to trim the sharp tips from the outer leaves or remove any tough leaves if you find it difficult to fit them all in your cooker.

3 Once you've got them in there, close the lid and the steam valve, and set it to high pressure for 8 minutes. Manually release the pressure.

4 Prepare the aioli of your choice by combining all of the ingredients listed for that particular aioli in a small bowl. Refrigerate until ready to use. After they have been chilled, you may need to add a little more almond or coconut milk to thin them out again.

5 Serve the artichokes with the aioli.

Basic Spaghetti Squash

Spaghetti squash can now fall into the category of "last-minute side dish" because it cooks so quickly in a pressure cooker! I include two ways to dress it up in the next couple of recipes, but if you're wanting something super simple, a sprinkle of salt and pepper and a few dabs of ghee or grass-fed butter is my go-to.

Prep time 5 minutes
Pressure time 7 minutes
Serves 3-4

1 medium spaghetti squash

1 Put 1 cup (235 ml) of water and the wire rack inside the pot.

2 Cut the spaghetti squash in half and scoop out the seeds and membranes.

3 Place the squash halves in the pot. Close the lid and the steam valve. Set the cooker to high pressure for 7 minutes. Manually release all of the pressure when it has finished.

4 Remove the squash with a pair of tongs and let it cool enough for you to handle it. Scrape out the squash "strings" with a fork.

5 Serve or cover and chill for later.

Note: If your squash is particularly large or small, you might want to add or take away a minute or two of cooking time.

Spaghetti Squash with Sun-Dried Tomato Pesto

I'm the only one in my family who loves chunks of sun-dried tomatoes in their meal. For the rest of my family to tolerate them, I buzz them up into a pesto and use it to add a rich tomato flavor—like in this squash. The pesto also makes fabulous omelets when you whisk a tablespoon (15 g) or so into your eggs before cooking.

Prep time 15 minutes
Pressure time 9 minutes
Serves 6

1 large spaghetti squash, cut in half and seeds scraped out
Sea salt and black pepper

For the pesto:
⅔ cup (73 g) oil-packed sun-dried tomatoes, drained

3 tablespoons (45 ml) olive oil from the sun-dried tomato jar
2 tablespoons (28 ml) red wine vinegar
1 tablespoon (9 g) pine nuts
1 clove garlic
8 large fresh basil leaves
Pinch of sea salt

1 Put 1 cup (235 ml) of water and the wire rack in the bottom of the pot.

2 Sprinkle the insides of the squash halves with a generous pinch of salt and pepper. Arrange the squash halves in the pot, stacking if needed.

3 Close the lid and the steam valve. Set the cooker to high pressure for 9 minutes. When it's finished, use a quick release to release all of the pressure.

4 Meanwhile, to make the pesto, put all of the pesto ingredients into a food processor or blender. Blend until smooth.

5 Scrape out the squash threads and put them in a serving bowl. Add 2-3 tablespoons (30-45 g) of pesto to the squash and toss to combine. Taste and add a pinch of salt if needed. Save the remaining pesto, chilled, for later use.

6 Serve the squash warm.

Spaghetti Squash Carbonara

Just four ingredients and you've got a rich, "cheesy" meal that is perfect for a busy weeknight evening. Tip: You can make the cheeze sauce ahead of time and warm it in a skillet over medium-low heat when you're ready to eat.

Prep time 20 minutes
Pressure time 7 minutes
Serves 4

10 ounces (280 g) uncooked bacon, cut into 1-inch (2.5 cm) pieces
1 medium spaghetti squash

1 cup (235 ml) Garlic Alfredo Sauce (page 240)
4 scallions, thinly sliced

1 Put the bacon in a large skillet and cook it over medium heat until crispy, about 20 minutes.

2 Meanwhile, put 1 cup (235 ml) of water in the pot and place the wire rack inside.

3 Cut the spaghetti squash in half crosswise and scoop out the seeds and membranes from the center. Place the squash halves in the cooker. Close the lid and the steam valve. Set the cooker to high pressure for 7 minutes. Release the pressure manually.

4 Remove the squash with tongs and wait a few minutes until it's cool enough to handle. Spread some paper towels out on a baking sheet. Scrape out the squash strands and spread them on the paper towels to soak up any excess moisture.

5 Serve the squash with a few spoonfuls of Garlic Alfredo Sauce, a sprinkle of bacon, and scallions.

Orange-Balsamic Beets

Orange goes well with beets. Orange also goes well with balsamic vinegar. It only makes sense that the three of them would get along beautifully. I love to make a big batch of these beets and keep them in the fridge to add to my lunch salads during the week.

Prep time 5 minutes
Pressure time 18 minutes
Serves 6

2 pounds (900 g) medium beets, tops trimmed off
Juice of 1 large navel orange (about ⅓ cup [80 ml])

½ cup (120 ml) balsamic vinegar
2 cloves of garlic, smashed
Pinch of sea salt

1 Put 1 cup (235 ml) of water and the wire rack in the pot. Put the beets on the wire rack.

2 Close the cooker and the steam valve. Set the cooker to high pressure for 18 minutes. If the beets are on the small side, reduce the time by 2–3 minutes. If they're bigger, add a couple of minutes. Use a quick release when the cooker has finished the pressure cycle.

3 Put the orange juice, vinegar, garlic, and salt in a small skillet. Simmer over medium heat for 10-15 minutes until it has reduced by half and thickened some.

4 Remove the beets from the pot and when they are cool enough to handle, rub them with a paper towel to remove the skins and then cut them into 1-inch (2.5 cm) chunks or wedges.

5 Toss the beets with the balsamic glaze and serve warm or at room temperature.

Roasted Cauliflower Rice

If you're ever bored of sautéed cauliflower rice, try roasting it in the oven! It adds a nice caramelized flavor. Luckily, pre-riced cauliflower is easy to find, so it's a snap to make a grain-free side dish in a hurry.

Prep time 15 minutes
Cook time 20-25 minutes
Serves 4

1 large head of cauliflower or the equivalent in pre-riced cauliflower

3 tablespoons (45 ml) avocado or coconut oil

¼ teaspoon sea salt

1 Preheat the oven to 425°F (220°C, or gas mark 7).

2 Remove the leaves and thick stems from the cauliflower and trim it down to 1- to 2-inch (2.5 to 5 cm) florets. Working in batches, pulse the florets in a food processor until they are the size of rice grains.

3 Transfer the minced cauliflower to a rimmed baking sheet. Drizzle with the oil and salt and using your hands, toss to ensure the cauliflower is coated evenly. Spread it out in an even layer on the pan.

4 Roast on a lower oven rack for 20-25 minutes, stirring once or twice, until the cauliflower is golden brown, or as brown as you prefer.

5 Transfer to a serving bowl and serve immediately.

Note: This can easily be doubled. Just use one head of cauliflower per baking sheet and rotate the pans halfway through roasting.

Cauliflower Puree with Rosemary and Garlic

I'm an Idaho girl at heart, and I'm pretty picky about mashed potatoes. The fact that I LOVED this cauliflower puree in place of mashed potatoes says a lot! They have so much delicious flavor with the rosemary and garlic added. And don't skimp on the ghee.

Prep time 10 minutes
Pressure time 10 minutes
Serves 8-10

3 medium heads of cauliflower

½ cup (120 ml) chicken broth, homemade (page 242) or store-bought

1 teaspoon sea salt

1 tablespoon (10 g) minced garlic

3 large sprigs of fresh rosemary or 1 teaspoon crushed dried rosemary

4 tablespoons (60 ml) ghee (page 234) or (112 g) grass-fed butter

Chopped fresh Italian flat-leaf parsley, for garnish (optional)

1 Trim the leaves and stems from the cauliflower and cut it into 1- to 2-inch (2.5 to 5 cm) pieces. Place them into the pot. (No need to use the rack.) It should be filled to the "Max" line, but no higher.

2 Add the chicken broth, salt, garlic, and rosemary to the pot.

3 Close the lid and the steam valve. Set it to high pressure for 10 minutes. Release the pressure manually when it is finished.

4 Remove the lid. Remove the rosemary sprigs, leaving a few leaves behind. Discard the stems. Add the ghee and stir it around until it melts.

5 Blend the cauliflower in batches (with the liquid) in a blender and transfer to a large serving dish. Taste and add a little extra salt if needed. Garnish with parsley.

SWEET ENDINGS

Pressure cookers are not just for quick weeknight meals or cooking eggs. You can make dessert in it, too! The benefit of making paleo-friendly baked goods in a steamy environment is that you end up with extra moist cakes and custards that have a built-in water bath. There is truly something for everyone in this section, whether you're having a group of friends over for movie night or are hosting a dinner party.

Recipes

Wassailed Cranberry Sauce

If you're looking for a naturally sweetened, no-fuss cranberry sauce, try using this recipe in your pressure cooker! I love the combination of citrus and spices in wassail and found it works wonderfully in cranberry sauce as well.

Prep time 5 minutes

Pressure time 5 minutes + 10 minutes natural release

Makes about 2½–3 cups (600–720 g)

12 ounces (340 g) fresh cranberries
½ cup (120 ml) unsweetened apple cider
1 cinnamon stick
1 orange

1 vanilla bean or 2 teaspoons vanilla extract

6 tablespoons (90 ml) pure maple syrup, (120 g) honey, or (90 g) Date Paste (page 232)

1 Place the cranberries, cider, and cinnamon stick in the pot.

2 Using a vegetable peeler, peel off 3 strips of the orange zest and put the strips into the pot. Cut the orange in half and squeeze half of the juice into the pot, too, about ¼ cup (60 ml).

3 Use a sharp knife to cut open the vanilla bean lengthwise and then use the back of the knife (the blunt edge) to scrape out the black seeds. Put the seeds and the pod into the pot along with the maple syrup.

4 Close the lid and the steam valve. Set the cooker to high pressure for 5 minutes. Let the pressure release naturally for 10 minutes before releasing the rest manually.

5 Remove the lid and let the sauce cool for several minutes. It should thicken as it cools off. Taste and adjust the sweetener if you feel it needs it. Remove the cinnamon stick.

6 Serve alongside your Thanksgiving dinner or on pancakes, waffles, or paleo-friendly ice cream.

Cran-Raspberry Applesauce

If you have kids who are anything like mine, you might also be buying applesauce in bulk. To change things up, I use my pressure cooker to make lightning-fast applesauce. Sometimes, I add berries (which I love!), but more often than not, my kids prefer it plain. I guess they're applesauce purists, but that doesn't stop me from making a batch of this Cran-Raspberry Applesauce for myself once in a while.

Prep time 10 minutes

Pressure time 3 minutes + 15 minutes natural release

Makes about 5 cups (1.2 kg)

½ cup (120 ml) unsweetened apple cider or juice

½ cup (55 g) fresh or frozen cranberries

1 cup (125 g) fresh or frozen raspberries

6 medium sweet apples of mixed varieties, cored and chopped into large pieces (peeling optional)

1 teaspoon vanilla extract

3-4 tablespoons (60-80 g) honey (if needed)

1 Put the cider, cranberries, raspberries, apple pieces, and vanilla in the pot.

2 Close the lid and the steam valve. Set the cooker to high heat for 3 minutes. Let the cooker release pressure naturally for 15 minutes and then release any remaining pressure manually.

3 Blend the applesauce with an immersion blender as smooth as you prefer. Taste and add a little honey if it tastes too tart.

4 Ladle into lidded containers and store chilled for up to 2 weeks.

Spiced Orange Nut and Seed Clusters

I have a weakness for candied nuts, but I don't like the overly sweet ones. This recipe is my new go-to that includes some warm baking spices and orange flavors to make them more interesting. You can also use these sweet clusters as a grain-free paleo granola.

Prep time 10 minutes
Pressure time 3 minutes + 5 minutes natural release + 10-15 minutes roasting
Makes about 4½ cups (563 g)

3 cups whole raw nuts ([300 g] pecans, [435 g] almond, [420 g] cashews, [300 g] walnuts)
⅓ cup (48 g) sunflower seeds
⅓ cup (46 g) raw pepitas (pumpkin seeds)
½ cup (120 ml) pure maple syrup
3 tablespoons (45 ml) melted coconut oil

1 tablespoon (7 g) ground cinnamon
½ teaspoon ground cardamom
¼ teaspoon sea salt
2 large naval or Cara-Cara oranges
1 cup (60 g) unsweetened coconut flakes

1 Put the nuts and seeds into the pot. Add the maple syrup, coconut oil, cinnamon, cardamom, and salt to the pot. Add the zest from one of the oranges and the juice from both oranges (about ½ cup [120 ml]). Give everything a good stir.

2 Close the lid and the steam valve. Set the cooker to high pressure for 3 minutes.

3 Meanwhile, preheat your oven to 350°F (180°C, or gas mark 4) and line a rimmed baking sheet with parchment paper.

4 Let the cooker release pressure naturally for 5 minutes before releasing the pressure manually. There should be a syrupy coating on the nuts, but it shouldn't be watery.

5 Transfer the nut mixture to the parchment paper. Roast in the oven for 10-15 minutes until the nuts are toasted and any liquid has cooked off, tossing the nuts around with a spatula a couple of times during cooking. The clusters will crisp up as they cool.

Banana Bread with Cacao Nibs

The benefit of baking paleo goods in a pressure cooker is how moist they turn out! I find paleo baked goods can easily be crumbly or have a strange chalky texture. Baking in a steamy environment helps remedy that.

Prep time 15 minutes

Pressure time 45 minutes + 5 minutes natural release

Serves 6

You'll need a 7-inch (18 cm) springform pan or a 2-inch (5 cm)-tall heat-safe casserole dish that will fit in your pressure cooker insert pot.

2 cups (450 g) mashed very ripe bananas (about 4 large bananas)

⅓ cup (80 ml) melted ghee (page 234), grass-fed butter, or coconut oil

2 eggs

1 tablespoon (15 ml) vanilla extract

⅔ cup (96 g) coconut sugar

1 cup (112 g) blanched almond flour

½ cup (56 g) coconut flour

1 teaspoon ground cinnamon

1 teaspoon baking soda

¼ teaspoon sea salt

⅓ cup (43 g) + 2 tablespoons (16 g) cacao nibs or mini dark chocolate chips, divided (91 g and 34 g)

1 In a large bowl, combine the mashed bananas, ghee, eggs, and vanilla extract. Stir in the coconut sugar until well combined.

2 Add the almond flour, coconut flour, cinnamon, baking soda, salt, and ⅓ cup (43 g) of the cacao nibs. Mix everything together well.

3 Prepare your pot by putting ½ cup (120 ml) of water and the wire rack inside. Prepare the springform pan by spraying it with nonstick spray.

4 Pour the batter into the spring-form pan and spread it evenly. Sprinkle the remaining 2 tablespoons (16 g) of cacao nibs over the top. Put the pan on the wire rack and close the lid and the steam valve on the cooker.

5 Set the cooker to high pressure for 45 minutes. Let the cooker release pressure on its own for 5 minutes before releasing the rest of the pressure manually.

6 Carefully lift the wire rack with the springform pan out of the cooker and onto a countertop to cool for 15 minutes. Unlatch the springform pan, cut the banana bread into wedges, and serve.

Brown Sugar Peach Mug Cakes

Coconut sugar reminds me a lot of brown sugar with its caramel notes and deep, sweet flavor. Those flavors pair well with peaches in these cute, individual serving cakes. You can use mugs if you like, but I find I can fit more regular-mouth pint (475 ml) canning jars in my pressure cooker at one time.

Prep time 15 minutes

Pressure time 15 minutes + 5 minutes natural release

Serves 6

You'll need six regular mouth 1 pint (475 ml) mason jars

1½ cups (168 g) almond flour

½ cup (60 g) tapioca flour

½ cup (72 g) coconut sugar, divided

½ teaspoon baking soda

1 teaspoon ground cinnamon, divided

¼ teaspoon sea salt

Pinch of ground nutmeg

⅓ cup (80 ml) coconut or almond milk

3 tablespoons (45 ml) melted coconut oil

1 egg + 1 egg yolk

1 tablespoon (15 ml) vanilla extract

4 cups (680 g) chopped peaches, fresh or frozen (no need to thaw)

1 In a medium bowl, whisk together the almond flour, tapioca flour, ¼ cup (36 g) of the coconut sugar, baking soda, ½ teaspoon of the cinnamon, salt, and nutmeg. In a separate, smaller bowl, whisk together the coconut milk, coconut oil, egg, egg yolk, and vanilla. Pour the wet mixture into the dry mixture and stir gently just until combined.

2 Prepare the mason jars with nonstick spray. Put the remaining ¼ cup (36 g) of coconut sugar and remaining ½ teaspoon of cinnamon in a small bowl.

3 Divide the peaches among the mason jars—they should each be filled about two-thirds full with peaches. Sprinkle 1 tablespoon (9 g) of the coconut sugar mixture into each jar over the peaches.

4 Divide the batter among the jars, putting roughly ¼ cup (60 ml) into each one. Top each mug with ½ teaspoon of coconut sugar mixture.

5 Put 1 cup (235 ml) of water and the wire rack in the bottom of the pot. Place the mason jars on the wire rack.

6 Close the lid and the steam valve and set the cooker to high pressure for 15 minutes. Let the pressure release naturally for 5 minutes and then release the remaining pressure manually.

7 Carefully remove the mason jars from the cooker and serve warm.

Note: If you use wide-mouth canning jars, you'll need to cook them in two batches.

Salted Caramel Coconut Flan

Flan (and anything pudding or custard related) is one of my husband's favorite desserts. I love that moment when you flip it upside down and see the caramelized syrup drip down the side of the custard. This is a great make-ahead recipe and the flans are good for a couple of days in the fridge before you serve them. Just don't flip them until you're ready to eat.

Prep time 20 minutes + 4 hours chilling time

Pressure time 10 minutes + 15 minutes natural release

Serves 6

You'll need six 6-ounce (175 ml) ramekins

Two 13.5-ounce (385 g) cans full-fat coconut milk

1 cup (144 g) coconut sugar, divided

Pinch of sea salt

2 tablespoons (28 ml) water

6 eggs

¼ teaspoon ground cinnamon

¼ teaspoon flaky sea salt (like Maldon)

1 Combine the coconut milk, ½ cup (72 g) of the coconut sugar, and salt in a medium saucepan over medium heat. Gently heat the mixture until it just barely bubbles and the sugar has dissolved, whisking often. Remove from the heat.

2 Meanwhile, start the caramel sauce by putting the remaining ½ cup (72 g) of coconut sugar and the water in a small skillet over medium-low heat. Bring the mixture to a boil, using a rubber spatula to scrape the bottom and sides of the pan often so the sugar doesn't burn. Let it bubble vigorously for about 30 seconds and then remove it from the heat.

3 Whisk the eggs together in a large bowl. While whisking, slowly drizzle in ½ cup (120 ml) of the heated coconut milk mixture to heat the eggs gently. Then, very slowly pour the rest of the coconut milk mixture into the egg mixture, whisking constantly. When everything is combined, set a fine-mesh strainer over the saucepan and pour the custard mixture through the strainer and back into the saucepan to catch any bits of egg that may have scrambled.

4 Divide the caramel sauce among the ramekins—about 1 tablespoon (15 ml) caramel per container.

Sprinkle a pinch of cinnamon and flaky sea salt in each ramekin. Then, divide the custard among the ramekins, filling them full or within ½ inch (1.3 cm) from the top of the ramekin. Cover each ramekin with a small piece of aluminum foil.

5 Put 1 cup (235 ml) of water and the wire rack in the bottom of the pressure cooker pot. Set 3 of the ramekins on the wire rack. Set another rack (or something similar) on the ramekins and stack the other 3 ramekins on top of that so all 6 ramekins are in the cooker.

6 Close the lid and the steam valve. Set the cooker to high pressure for 10 minutes. Let the cooker release pressure naturally for 15 minutes before releasing any remaining pressure manually.

7 Carefully remove the ramekins from the cooker and let them sit at room temperature until they can be handled with bare hands. Transfer them to the refrigerator to chill for at least 4 hours. You can make these up to 4 days in advance if you like.

8 To serve, remove the foil and invert the ramekin onto a small dessert plate or shallow bowl.

Whipped Coconut Cream

While we do still splurge sometimes and use real whipped cream, it's nice to have a dairy-free option if you don't tolerate dairy well, or at all. I love the coconut flavor it adds, too!

Prep time 5 minutes
Makes about 1½ cups (120 g)

Two or three 13.5-ounce (385 g) cans full-fat coconut milk, chilled

1 Open the cans from the bottom and drain out the clear-ish liquid. (You can save it for smoothies.)

2 Scoop out the hardened coconut cream and place it into a medium bowl. Whip the cream using a hand-held mixer until soft and fluffy. Blend in the sweetener and vanilla extract. Taste and adjust the sweetener if needed.

1 tablespoon preferred sweetener ([20 g] honey, [3 g] stevia, or [15 ml] maple syrup), or to taste
¼ teaspoon vanilla extract (optional)

3 Chill until ready to use, but if you chill it too long, it will harden and you'll have to whip it again to loosen it up.

Note: The creaminess of coconut milk varies among brands, so you may need three cans in order to get enough coconut cream. You could also purchase cans of coconut cream to get more cream per can.

Spiced Apple Cobbler

Using more than one type of apple is one of the secrets to a flavorful apple dessert. I like to use mostly tart and tart-sweet varieties if the rest of the dessert has a lot of sweetness in it. My favorite part of this recipe is how the apples cook down and create a velvety cinnamon sauce that gets soaked up by the cakelike cobbler. Don't forget the Whipped Coconut Cream (page 211)!

Prep time 15 minutes
Pressure time 15 minutes + 10 minutes natural release
Serves 8

For the filling:

2½ pounds (1.1 kg) tart baking apples, cored and sliced into ¼-inch (6 mm) pieces (about 4 large apples, peeling optional)

2 tablespoons (28 ml) freshly squeezed lemon juice

1 tablespoon (8 g) tapioca flour

½ teaspoon ground cinnamon

⅓ cup (48 g) coconut sugar

½ cup (120 ml) water

For the topping:

1 cup (112 g) blanched almond flour

¾ cup (90 g) tapioca flour

⅓ cup (48 g) coconut sugar

2 teaspoons ground cinnamon

½ teaspoon ground cloves

Pinch of sea salt

½ cup (104 g) palm shortening

1 egg

½ cup (46 g) sliced almonds

1 To make the filling, place the apples into the pot and sprinkle the lemon juice over the apples.

2 Stir together the tapioca flour, cinnamon, and coconut sugar. Sprinkle the mixture over the apples and stir them to coat everything evenly. Pour the water into the center of the pot.

3 To make the topping, combine the almond flour, tapioca, coconut sugar, cinnamon, cloves, and salt in a food processor. Pulse until combined.

4 Add the palm shortening by spoonfuls, pulsing a few times in between additions. Continue to pulse until the mixture resembles wet sand.

5 Add the egg and pulse until a dough forms and wedges itself into one side of the processor bowl.

6 Add the dough to the apples in spoonfuls, scattered evenly over the top. You do not need to spread it around. Sprinkle the sliced almonds on top.

7 Close the lid and the steam valve and set it to high pressure for 15 minutes. Let the pressure release naturally for 10 minutes and then release the rest of the pressure manually, if you wish.

8 Remove the lid and let the cobbler cool for 10–15 minutes before serving.

9 Serve with paleo-friendly ice cream or Whipped Coconut Cream.

Note: If you don't have a food processor, just whisk the dry ingredients together in a bowl and use a fork to cut the shortening into the dry mixture. Then, add the egg to form a dough and proceed with the recipe.

Crustless Chai Pumpkin Pie Cups with Toasted Marshmallow Fluff

I recently discovered how versatile Chai Spice Blend (page 245) can be and how close it is in flavor to pumpkin pie spice with a slightly more exotic flavor. If you don't want to make the chai blend, you can definitely use pumpkin pie spice here. Just make sure it's fresh and hasn't been in the cupboard since the early '90s. (C'mon, we've all done it.)

Prep time 15 minutes + 4 hour chilling time

Pressure time 8 minutes + 15 minutes natural release

Serves 6

You'll need six 6-ounce (175 ml) ramekins or heat-safe glass bowls.

6 egg yolks

⅔ cup (96 g) coconut sugar

1 cup (245 g) pumpkin puree

1 cup (235 ml) unsweetened almond or coconut milk

2 teaspoons Chai Spice Blend (see page 245) or pumpkin pie spice

Pinch of sea salt

1 recipe Low-Carb Marshmallow Fluff (page 226) or Whipped Coconut Cream (page 211), for serving

1 Whisk together all of the ingredients (except the Low-Carb Marshmellow Fluff) in a medium bowl or a large glass measuring cup.

2 Prepare the ramekins with nonstick spray. Pour about ½ cup (120 ml) of the mixture into each ramekin. Cover each ramekin tightly with a small piece of aluminum foil.

3 Put 1 cup (235 ml) of water and the wire rack in the pot. Put 3 ramekins on the rack. If you have another similar rack, place it on top of the ramekins and stack the other 3 ramekins on top.

4 Close the lid and the steam valve. Set the cooker to high pressure for 8 minutes. Let the cooker release pressure naturally for 15 minutes before releasing any remaining pressure manually.

5 Carefully remove the ramekins from the cooker and let them sit, covered, until they're cool enough to handle. Transfer them to the fridge and chill for at least 4 hours or until completely cold.

6 Top each ramekin with a big spoonful of Low-Carb Marshmallow Fluff and toast it with a handheld kitchen torch or under an oven broiler for just a few minutes. If you use the Whipped Coconut Cream, don't toast it or it'll melt.

Nut-Free Tahini-Swirled Brownies

Developing this recipe was my first experience with adding tahini to sweet baked goods. I'm totally hooked! When mixed with chocolate, tahini takes on a peanut-like flavor. That's good news for all of the peanut butter lovers who are trying to avoid legumes!

Prep time 15 minutes

Pressure time 15 minutes + 5 minutes natural release

Serves 6

You'll need a 7-inch (18 cm) springform pan or 7-inch (18 cm) round cake pan.

1 cup (120 g) tapioca flour

⅓ cup (27 g) unsweetened cocoa powder or cacao powder

2 tablespoons (14 g) coconut flour

½ teaspoon baking soda

¼ teaspoon sea salt

½ cup preferred sweetener ([170 g] honey, [120 ml] maple syrup, or [72 g] coconut sugar)

⅓ cup (80 g) + 2 tablespoons (30 g) tahini, divided

1 egg

¼ cup (60 ml) melted ghee (page 234) or (55 g) grass-fed butter

¼ cup (32 g) cacao nibs (optional)

1 Line the bottom of a 7-inch (18 cm) round baking pan with parchment paper and spray the whole pan with nonstick spray.

2 In a medium bowl, whisk together the tapioca flour, cocoa powder, coconut flour, baking soda, and salt.

3 Add the sweetener, ⅓ cup (80 g) of the tahini, the egg, and the ghee. Add them all to the bowl with the dry ingredients and THEN stir it well.

4 Pour the batter into the prepared baking pan. Drizzle the remaining 2 tablespoons (30 g) of tahini on top of the batter in a swirling fashion and then sprinkle the cacao nibs on top (if using).

5 Place the wire rack inside the pot and add 1 cup (235 ml) of water. Put the baking pan on top of the wire rack.

6 Close the lid and the steam valve. Set the cooker to high pressure for 15 minutes. Let the pressure release naturally for 5 minutes before manually releasing the rest of the pressure.

7 Transfer the rack and the baking pan to a countertop to cool for a few minutes.

8 Run a knife around the inside edge of the baking pan and then invert the pan onto a plate. Place another plate upside down on the brownies and flip again to turn them right side up.

9 Slice and serve warm or cold.

Peppermint Pots de Crème

If you need a fancy, rich dessert for a dinner party (that also needs to be dairy-free), make these dark chocolate pudding cups! You can also make them a couple of days in advance so you can spend your time visiting with guests instead of prepping dessert.

Prep time 20 minutes + 4-24 hours chilling time

Pressure time 6 minutes + 15 minutes natural release

Serves 6

You'll need six half-pint (235 ml) mason jars or 6-ounce (175 ml) ramekins.

2 cups (475 ml) unsweetened almond milk or full-fat coconut milk

5 egg yolks

¼ cup (36 g) coconut sugar

Pinch of sea salt

8 ounces (225 g) dark 70% cacao chocolate chips

½ teaspoon peppermint extract or 2–3 drops peppermint essential oil

Whipped Coconut Cream (page 211), for serving (optional)

1 Put the milk in a medium saucepan. Heat over medium heat until steamy, but not boiling. Remove from the heat.

2 Put the yolks in a medium bowl and whisk in the coconut sugar and salt. Slowly whisk about ¼ cup (60 ml) of the warm milk mixture into the egg yolks to warm them gently and then slowly whisk the rest of the milk mixture into the bowl with the eggs.

3 Put a fine-mesh sieve over the saucepan and then pour the egg-milk mixture through it, back into the saucepan. Immediately add the chocolate chips and let it sit for 5 minutes.

4 Whisk the mixture to blend the chocolate thoroughly. Add the peppermint.

5 Divide the custard into six half-pint (235 ml) mason jars (filled half full) or 6-ounce (175 ml) ramekins (filled two-thirds full). Cover each container with a small piece of foil.

6 Put 1 cup (235 ml) of water and the wire rack into the pressure cooker pot. If you're using the narrow-mouth mason jars, you can fit them all in one layer. If you're using the wide-mouth mason jars or ramekins, put 3 on the wire rack, top with another wire rack, and then put the other 3 on top of that.

7 Close the lid and the steam valve. Set the cooker to high pressure for 6 minutes. Let the cooker release pressure for 15 minutes naturally and then release any remaining pressure manually.

8 Remove the custards from the pot. Let the custards cool until you can handle them with your bare hands and then transfer them to the refrigerator. Chill for at least 4 hours, up to 24 hours.

9 Serve the custards with a dollop of Whipped Coconut Cream, if desired.

"Peanut" Butter Cup Lava Cakes

Do you feel a little giddy when you poke a lava cake and see the gooey center ooze out? Or am I the only one who turns into a six-year-old when I eat desserts like this? Either way, the nut butter–chocolate combo is always a hit with me.

Prep time 20 minutes
Pressure time 7 minutes
Serves 4

You'll need four 6-ounce (175 ml) ramekins or heat-safe glass bowls.

1 cup (175 g) dark 70% cacao chocolate chips

½ cup (120 ml) melted ghee (page 234), grass-fed butter, or coconut oil

½ cup (72 g) coconut sugar

3 eggs

1 egg yolk

1 teaspoon vanilla extract

⅓ cup (40 g) cassava flour or tapioca flour

2 teaspoons coconut flour

Pinch of sea salt

4 tablespoons (64 g) nut butter (any kind)

1 Put the chocolate chips and ghee in a small saucepan and gently heat over medium-low heat until the chocolate is mostly melted. Remove the pan from the heat and whisk to melt the chocolate the rest of the way.

2 Add the coconut sugar and whisk vigorously until the sugar has dissolved and the mixture is no longer grainy. Whisk in the eggs one at a time, as well as the egg yolk and the vanilla.

3 Stir in the cassava flour, coconut flour, and salt.

4 Prepare four 6-ounce (175 ml) ramekins or oven-safe glass bowls with nonstick spray. Put about ⅓ cup (80 ml) of batter into each container. Put 1 tablespoon (16 g) of nut butter in the center of each ramekin and then top with the remaining batter to cover the nut butter in each ramekin.

5 Put 1 cup (235 ml) of water and the wire rack in the pressure cooker pot. You'll probably need to put 2 or 3 ramekins on the bottom with another wire rack on top and then the other ramekins on top of the second rack. You could also cook them in two batches.

6 Once the ramekins are in place, close the lid and the steam valve. Set the cooker to high pressure for 7 minutes. Once it is finished, use a quick release to release all the pressure manually.

7 Remove the ramekins from the pot and invert them onto serving dishes. Serve immediately while still warm and the centers will be lava-like.

Note: These are great with a scoop of paleo-friendly ice cream or some Whipped Coconut Cream (page 211).

Dark Chocolate and Strawberry Layer Cake

As a self-proclaimed chocolate cake snob, I was pleasantly surprised at the rich, chocolaty flavor and pound cake–like texture of this grain-free cake. The dark chocolate buttercream and strawberries give it a chocolate-covered strawberry kind of feel. It's a wonderful little cake for a celebration or a birthday!

Prep time 15 minutes + cooling time

Pressure time 40 minutes + 10 minutes natural release

Serves 6-8

You'll need a 7-inch (18 cm) springform pan or 7-inch (18 cm) round cake pan.

For the cake:

2½ cups (280 g) blanched almond flour

½ cup (60 g) tapioca flour

½ cup (40 g) cocoa powder

¼ cup (36 g) coconut sugar

1 teaspoon baking soda

¼ teaspoon sea salt

½ cup (120 ml) pure maple syrup

⅓ cup (80 ml) melted coconut oil or ghee (page 234)

¼ cup (60 ml) coconut or almond milk

3 eggs

1 teaspoon vanilla extract

1 pound (455 g) strawberries, greens trimmed and thinly sliced

For the frosting:

½ cup (104 g) palm shortening (or ¼ cup [52 g] palm shortening and ¼ cup [55 g] grass-fed butter)

¼ cup (20 g) unsweetened cocoa powder

¼ cup (60 ml) pure maple syrup

1 teaspoon vanilla extract

Pinch of sea salt

1 To make the cake, in a large bowl, whisk together the almond flour, tapioca flour, cocoa powder, coconut sugar, baking soda, and salt.

2 In a smaller bowl, whisk together the maple syrup, coconut oil, milk, eggs, and vanilla. Add the wet ingredients to the dry ingredients and stir just until combined.

3 Prepare a 7-inch (18 cm) springform pan or 7-inch (18 cm) round cake pan with nonstick spray. Pour the batter into the pan and smooth the top.

4 Put 1 cup (235 ml) of water and the wire rack into the pot.

5 Put the baking pan on the wire rack and close the lid and the steam valve. Set the cooker to high pressure for 40 minutes. Let the pressure release naturally for 10 minutes and then release any remaining pressure manually.

6 Remove the cake from the pressure cooker and let it cool for about 5 minutes before releasing the springform ring. Let the cake cool completely before proceeding.

continued

Notes:

- *If you're using a regular 7-inch (18 cm) baking pan, I recommend lining the bottom with a circle of parchment paper so the cake comes out more easily.*

- *If you prefer to frost the entire cake with the frosting, use just one-third of the frosting in the center.*

- *I also recommend the Low-Carb Marshmallow Fluff (page 226) as a frosting for this cake.*

7 To make the frosting, combine all of the frosting ingredients in a mixing bowl and beat for 2–3 minutes with a handheld mixer, scraping down the sides occasionally, until the frosting is smooth and has fluffed up a bit. Taste and add a little more maple syrup if you wish it to be sweeter. The frosting should have a dark chocolate flavor.

8 Transfer the cake to a large plate (removing it from the bottom part of the pan) and slice it in half horizontally to form two equal-size layers. Remove the top layer and spread half of the frosting on top of the remaining layer. Arrange enough strawberries on the frosting to cover it in one layer. Pile the rest of the frosting on top of the cake and spread evenly. Arrange the rest of the sliced strawberries nicely on the top of the cake.

Orange-Scented Carrot Cake with Marshmallow Frosting

It seems almost blasphemous to have a carrot cake without cream cheese frosting, but trust me—marshmallow frosting holds its own. Especially when you take a kitchen torch to it.

Prep time 20 minutes + cooling time
Pressure time 40 minutes + 10 minutes natural release
Serves 8

Notes:

- *If you're using a regular 7-inch (18 cm) baking pan, I recommend lining the bottom with a circle of parchment paper so the cake comes out more easily.*

- *If you prefer to frost the entire cake with the frosting, use just one-third of the frosting in the center.*

You'll need a 7-inch (18 cm) springform pan.

2½ cups (280 g) blanched almond flour
½ cup (60 g) tapioca flour
¼ cup (36 g) coconut sugar
1 teaspoon baking soda
1 teaspoon ground cinnamon
¼ teaspoon sea salt
Pinch of ground nutmeg
3 eggs
1½ cups (165 g) grated carrot
½ cup (120 ml) pure maple syrup
⅓ cup (80 ml) melted coconut oil or ghee (page 234)
¼ cup (60 ml) coconut milk or unsweetened almond milk
1 teaspoon vanilla extract
Zest from 1 large navel orange
½ cup (55 g) chopped pecans (optional)
1 recipe Low-Carb Marshmallow Fluff (page 226)

1 Combine the almond flour, tapioca flour, coconut sugar, baking soda, cinnamon, salt, and nutmeg in a medium bowl. In another medium bowl, combine the eggs, carrot, maple syrup, coconut oil, coconut milk, vanilla, and orange zest. Pour the wet mixture into the dry mixture and gently stir until just combined. If you're using the pecans, fold them in now.

2 Prepare a 7-inch (18 cm) springform pan with nonstick spray and transfer the batter to the pan. Spread it around evenly.

3 Put 1 cup (235 ml) of water and the wire rack in the pot. Put the springform pan on the wire rack and close the lid and the steam valve.

4 Set the cooker to high pressure for 40 minutes. Let the pressure release naturally for 10 minutes before releasing any remaining pressure manually.

5 Carefully lift the cake and rack out of the pot and let it cool for 5 minutes or so before releasing the springform ring. Let the cake cool completely before proceeding.

6 Transfer the cake to a large plate (removing it from the bottom part of the pan) and slice it in half horizontally to form two equal-size layers. Remove the top layer and spread half of the Low-Carb Marshmallow Fluff on top of the remaining layer. Put the other cake layer on top and pile the rest of the fluff on top of the cake. If you like, you can toast the marshmallow frosting with a kitchen torch before serving.

7 Serve using a sharp, serrated knife for slicing.

Dark Chocolate Chunk Cookie Wedges

I was doubtful about the texture of this cookie-cake concoction that I pulled out of my pressure cooker for the first time. When you bake in the pressure cooker, it's hard to get used to the ultra moist texture of the top of whatever you're baking. After it had completely cooled and I had a chance to inspect my creation, I was pleasantly surprised at the dense, slightly chewy texture, which happens to be my favorite texture for a cookie. And then I proceeded to eat half of the pan.

Prep time 15 minutes+ cooling time

Pressure time 40 minutes + 10 minutes natural release

Serves 8

You'll need a 7-inch (18 cm) springform pan or 7-inch (18 cm) round baking pan.

2½ cups (280 g) blanched almond flour

½ cup (60 g) tapioca flour

¼ cup (36 g) coconut sugar

1 teaspoon baking soda

¼ teaspoon sea salt

1 egg

½ cup (120 ml) pure maple syrup

¼ cup (60 ml) coconut milk or unsweetened almond milk

1 tablespoon (15 ml) vanilla extract

½ cup (85 g) chopped dark 70% cacao chocolate

1 In a large bowl, whisk together the almond flour, tapioca flour, coconut sugar, baking soda, and salt.

2 In a smaller bowl, whisk together the egg, maple syrup, coconut milk, and vanilla. Add the wet ingredients to the dry ingredients and stir just until combined. Fold in the chocolate chunks.

3 Prepare a 7-inch (18 cm) springform pan or 7-inch (18 cm) round baking pan by spraying it with nonstick spray. If you're using a regular baking pan, I recommend lining the bottom with a round piece of parchment paper as well.

4 Transfer the dough to the pan and spread it evenly.

5 Put 1 cup (235 ml) of water and the wire rack in the pot. Place the baking pan on the wire rack.

6 Set the cooker to high pressure for 40 minutes. Let the cooker release pressure naturally for 10 minutes before releasing any remaining pressure manually.

7 Carefully lift the pan out of the cooker and let it cool for at least 5 minutes before releasing the springform ring. (If you're using a regular baking pan, let it cool for 15 minutes before inverting the pan onto a plate to release the cookie.)

8 For best flavor and texture, let it cool completely before slicing into wedges and serving.

Low-Carb Marshmallow Fluff

I found that granulated low-carb sweeteners like xylitol and erythritol work much better in this recipe than natural sweeteners, like maple syrup or honey. That's great news for someone who is watching their carbs! I highly recommend using a kitchen torch to toast the marshmallow fluff.

Prep time 10 minutes
Makes about 2½ cups (260 g)

2 egg whites
⅓ cup (64 g) low-carb granulated sweetener, like xylitol or erythritol

⅛ teaspoon cream of tartar
1 teaspoon vanilla extract
Pinch of sea salt

1 Put the egg whites, sweetener, and cream of tartar in a large heat-safe bowl. Place the bowl in a saucepan with an inch or two (2.5 to 5 cm) of water in the bottom. Cook over medium-high heat, whisking, until the sweetener is dissolved and the mixture is warm to the touch.

2 Transfer the bowl to a flat work surface and beat with a handheld mixture for 5-7 minutes until the whites are fluffy and soft peaks form. Add the vanilla and salt and beat until combined.

3 Use the Low-Carb Marshmellow Fluff immediately.

BASICS AND PANTRY STAPLES

The foundation of paleo cooking (or any cooking, really) is great basics and pantry staples. I've collected a few of my favorite spice blend recipes, barbecue sauces, homemade broth, and even a recipe for homemade ghee! Yes, you can make your own, and it's much easier than you think.

Recipes

Paleo-Friendly Mayonnaise

Homemade mayonnaise is a game changer for me. I was never a fan of the taste of commercial mayo, and homemade has a mild flavor that's perfect for making aioli and adding a creamy component to recipes.

Total time 10 minutes
Makes about 1 cup (225 g)

2 egg yolks (from clean, fresh eggs, preferably pasture-raised)

3 tablespoons (45 ml) freshly squeezed lemon juice (about ½ large lemon)

½ teaspoon dry mustard

¾ teaspoon sea salt

½ clove garlic (optional)

1 cup (235 ml) avocado or light olive oil

1 Place the yolks, lemon juice, dry mustard, salt, and garlic in a food processor. Blend until smooth.

2 While the machine is running, slowly drizzle in the oil through the feed tube. The mixture should thicken quite a bit. Do not continue to blend after you are finished drizzling in the oil.

3 Transfer the mayonnaise to an airtight container. Taste and add more salt or lemon juice if needed. Store chilled for up to a week.

Notes:

• *I like to add a little garlic in my mayonnaise because it gives it more flavor. If you prefer to leave it out, please do.*

• *I like my mayo thick, which is why I use two egg yolks. To make a looser mayonnaise, use one.*

Paleo Pesto

Paleo pesto is simply regular pesto without the Parmesan cheese. And it's so easy to make! If you're still wanting a cheesy flavor, try adding a tablespoon (4 g) of nutritional yeast.

Prep time 15 minutes
Makes about ⅔ cup (160 g)

2 packed cups (48 g) fresh basil leaves (1 large or 2 small bunches)
⅓ cup (45 g) pine nuts
2 tablespoons (28 ml) freshly squeezed lemon juice

½ clove garlic, smashed
½ teaspoon sea salt
¼ teaspoon black pepper
⅓ cup (80 ml) extra-virgin olive oil

1 Place all of the ingredients (except the olive oil) in a food processor. Pulse until everything is minced well and combined.

2 While the machine is running, drizzle in the olive oil. Let it run for another 10 seconds or so until it is thoroughly blended. Scrape down the sides and pulse a few more times if necessary.

3 Transfer to an airtight container and use right away or cover and chill. It should keep for 4–5 days.

Date Paste

This simple sweetener using only dates was a lifesaver during my rounds of the Whole30 program, part of which omits all sweeteners from your diet for a short time. I used date paste to balance the acidity in vinaigrettes and tomato-based sauces, but you can use it as a substitute for maple syrup or honey in a recipe. Just remember that date paste is a lot thicker, so you may need to add more moisture if you're using it in a baking recipe.

Prep time: 5 minutes + soaking time
Makes about 1¼ cups (300 g)

20 Medjool dates, pitted

1 Place the dates in a bowl and cover with warm water. Let them soak for about 3 hours.

2 Drain the dates and transfer them to a blender or food processor. Puree until smooth.

3 Store in an airtight container (like a mason jar) in the refrigerator for up to 2 weeks.

Homemade Ghee

Ghee, or clarified butter, is butter that has had the milk solids removed. This allows the oil that is left over to be heated to higher temperatures without burning. Ghee is one of my favorite cooking fats—it has a nutty, buttery flavor and is great for sautéing, roasting, or drizzling as a finishing oil. You can purchase ghee in some stores or online, but making it is incredibly easy and less expensive if you find high-quality, grass-fed butter on sale—like the brand Kerrygold.

Cook time 15–20 minutes
Makes about 3½ cups (825 ml)

2 pounds (900 g) grass-fed butter (organic, if possible), such as Kerrygold brand

1 Cut the butter into large pieces and put it into a medium saucepan.

2 Cook the butter over medium-low heat until it is all melted.

3 Continue to cook the butter over medium-low heat. The butter will bubble and simmer for several minutes and get very foamy at the top. Then, the foam will subside and the top will be relatively clear. Then, after a few more minutes, it will get foamy again with smaller bubbles. At this point, remove the pan from the heat and use a spoon to skim the foam from the top. Do not scrape the residue from the bottom of the pot.

4 Pour the clear ghee into a lidded glass container for storage. Allow the ghee to cool completely and store, covered, at room temperature for a few days or chilled for a few weeks.

Mango-Chile BBQ Sauce

This is a fruity, slightly spicy take on BBQ sauce that has an island sort of feel. It's especially good on the Mango BBQ Pulled Pork recipe on page 154.

Prep time   15 minutes
Cook time   15 minutes
Makes   about 4 cups (940 ml)

2 tablespoons (28 ml) avocado oil

2 fresh chiles (Anaheim, poblano, jalapeño, etc.), seeded and diced

½ cup (80 g) chopped sweet onion

1 teaspoon minced garlic

½ cup (120 ml) water

One 14-ounce (395 g) can tomato sauce

1½ cups (262 g) frozen mango chunks or 1 fresh mango, diced

⅔ cup (160 ml) rice vinegar

⅓ cup (80 g) Date Paste (page 232) or (115 g) honey, to taste

Juice from 1 large lime (about 2 tablespoons [28 ml])

2 teaspoons chili powder

1 teaspoon smoked paprika

½ teaspoon liquid smoke

¼ teaspoon dried chipotle powder

1 Heat the avocado oil in a medium saucepan over medium-high heat.

2 Add the diced chiles and onion. Cook, stirring a few times, until the vegetables are soft, about 5 minutes. Add the garlic and cook until fragrant, about 30 seconds.

3 Add the rest of the ingredients. Simmer for 15–20 minutes.

4 Blend using an immersion blender or a countertop blender.

5 Store in an airtight container, chilled. Use within 2–3 weeks.

Dry Ranch Seasoning Mix

This is one of the first seasonings I started making from scratch. I was trying to wean myself off of those little green packets, and although it has a different flavor, it totally hits the spot. I almost always have a jar of it in the cupboard.

Makes about ⅓ cup (7 g)

1 tablespoon dried parsley

2 teaspoons freeze-dried chives

1½ teaspoons dried dill

1 teaspoon dry mustard

½ teaspoon paprika

½ teaspoon dried onion flakes

½ teaspoon garlic powder

½ teaspoon onion powder

½ teaspoon sea salt

Freshly ground black pepper

1 Shake the ingredients together in an airtight container.

2 Store at room temperature.

Note: To make Paleo-Friendly Ranch Dressing, combine 1 cup (235 g) Paleo-Friendly Mayonnaise (page 230), 1–2 tablespoons (1–2 g) Dry Ranch Seasoning Mix, a squeeze of fresh lemon juice, a pinch of salt, and enough almond milk to reach the desired consistency.

Paleo Teriyaki Sauce

Making homemade, paleo-friendly teriyaki sauce is much easier than it sounds. You can have this whipped up in the time it takes to gather your ingredients to begin dinner prep.

Prep time 10 minutes
Cook time 5 minutes
Makes about 1 cup (235 ml)

⅔ cup (160 ml) coconut aminos
½ cup (120 ml) water
3 tablespoons (45 ml) rice vinegar
2 teaspoons minced garlic
2 teaspoons finely grated ginger

2 teaspoons fish sauce
A pinch of crushed red pepper flakes (if you'd like it to have a little heat)
2 teaspoons tapioca or arrowroot flour

1 Put all the ingredients into a small saucepan. Simmer for 3-4 minutes, whisking often, until the sauce has thickened and the flavors have combined.

2 Store in an airtight container in the refrigerator for up to a week.

Note: Some brands of coconut aminos are sweeter than others. If you find you'd like the sauce to be sweeter, add a teaspoon or two of honey or until it's as sweet as you prefer.

Smoky Maple BBQ Sauce

This is a great basic BBQ sauce with lots of smoky flavor and sweetness from maple and molasses. Use it in any recipe that calls for BBQ sauce.

Prep time 10 minutes
Cook time 15 minutes
Makes about 4 cups (940 ml)

One 15-ounce (425 g) can tomato sauce
½ cup (120 ml) red wine vinegar
⅓ cup (80 ml) chicken broth, homemade (page 242) or store-bought, or vegetable broth
¼ cup (80 g) molasses

¼ cup (60 ml) pure maple syrup
2 tablespoons (30 g) Dijon mustard
1 tablespoon (8 g) chili powder
½ teaspoon chipotle chile powder
¼ teaspoon ground cumin

1 Combine all of the ingredients in a medium saucepan. Simmer for 15 minutes, stirring occasionally.

2 Store in a lidded container in the refrigerator. Use within 2-3 weeks.

Paleo Cashew Cheeze Sauce, Two Ways

I feel like I'm (fashionably?) late to the cashew cheese sauce party. Honestly, I was dubious of the whole idea, but had I known you could create such bold, creamy flavors from a bowl of soaked cashews, I would have arrived much sooner.

I include two versions in this recipe—a Garlic Alfredo Sauce and a Spicy Nacho Sauce. Feel free to adjust the flavors how you like or use the base recipe to create your own flavor!

Prep time   10 minutes + soaking time
Makes   about 1½ cups (355 ml)

Base recipe:

1 cup (140 g) raw, unsalted cashews (whole or pieces)

½ cup (120 ml) water

3 tablespoons (45 ml) freshly squeezed lemon juice

3 tablespoons (12 g) nutritional yeast

1 clove garlic

1 teaspoon onion powder

1 teaspoon sea salt

1 Put the cashews in a medium bowl and cover completely with steaming hot water. Let the cashews soak for at least an hour. Drain off the liquid.

2 Put the cashews in a blender or food processor along with the rest of the ingredients. Blend until smooth.

Garlic Alfredo Sauce

2 cloves of garlic

1 tablespoon (15 ml) melted ghee (page 234) or grass-fed butter

1 base recipe (above)

To make the Garlic Alfredo version, add the garlic and ghee to the base recipe and blend again. Serve warm as a dip or add it to a recipe to create a creamy, cheesy flavor. Use in Spaghetti Squash Carbonara (page 197), Chicken Alfredo with Broccoli and Leeks (page 134), or Chicken Cordon Bleu with Creamy Garlic Sauce (page 136).

Spicy Nacho Sauce

⅛–¼ teaspoon chipotle chile powder

⅛ teaspoon turmeric

1 base recipe (above)

To make the Spicy Nacho version, add the chipotle powder and turmeric to the base recipe and blend again. Use in Chili Cheeze Dip (page 18), BBQ Pork–Stuffed Peppers with Nacho Cheeze Sauce (page 92), or Tex-Mex Meatloaf with Nacho Cheeze Sauce (page 116).

Homemade Chicken or Beef Broth

I've been making homemade broth for almost 10 years now—mostly in my stock pot, but sometimes in a slow cooker. When I learned I could do the same thing in a pressure cooker in two hours that it took 18–24 before, my head nearly exploded. In a good way. The batches are smaller than what you can make in a stock pot, but it's much easier and quicker using a pressure cooker.

Prep time 10 minutes

Pressure time 120 minutes + 15 minutes natural release

Makes 3–3½ quarts (2.8–3.3 L) if using a 6-quart (5.7 L) pressure cooker

1 meaty carcass from a 4- to 5-pound (1.8–2.3 kg) whole chicken (or the equivalent in miscellaneous chicken bones) or 2–3 pounds (908–1365 g) beef bones

1 large onion, quartered

2–3 celery stalks, cut into large pieces

2–3 carrots, cut into large pieces

Large handful of fresh herbs (like thyme, sage, parsley, or rosemary)

1 tablespoon (10 g) whole black peppercorns

2 bay leaves

2 cloves of garlic, peeled

1 Place all of the ingredients into your pressure cooker. You won't need the rack for this. Fill the cooker with water up to the maximum fill line.

2 Close the lid and the steam valve and set the cooker to high pressure for 120 minutes. Allow the cooker to release pressure naturally for 15 minutes before releasing the remaining pressure manually.

3 Remove the bones and large vegetable pieces with tongs or a spider skimmer and discard them. Pour the rest of the stock through a large fine-mesh strainer into a very large bowl. Let the stock cool until it reaches room temperature.

4 If you aren't using the stock right away, transfer it to containers for chilled storage. For freezing, I like to use quart-size (1 L) plastic containers. You can also use mason jars, leaving a couple inches (5 cm) of headspace, or zip-top freezer bags.

Chorizo Seasoning

This recipe was created during an attempt to re-create the pork and chicken chorizo at Chipotle restaurant. The spice blend I threw together was so delicious, I found more uses for it! I love the blend of all of the types of paprika—I think that's what sets it apart from other Tex-Mex seasoning blends. If you can't find hot Hungarian paprika, add another 1½ teaspoons of both sweet and smoked paprika and increase the dried chipotle powder by ⅛ teaspoon.

Makes a scant ½ cup (50 g)

2 tablespoons (14 g) sweet paprika

1 tablespoon (7 g) hot Hungarian paprika

1 tablespoon (7 g) smoked paprika

1 tablespoon (15 g) sea salt

2 teaspoons dried oregano

½–1 teaspoon dried chipotle chile powder (depending on how spicy you want it)

1 teaspoon freshly ground black pepper

1 teaspoon ground cumin

1 teaspoon garlic powder or granulated garlic

Mix all of the spices and store in an airtight container.

Middle Eastern Seasoning

My sweet cousin used to send me spice blends years ago—she knows the way to my heart. One of them was this Middle Eastern blend that uses seasonings that are easy to find. I loved it so much I kept refilling my jar and now it has a permanent place in my spice collection.

Makes about ⅔ cup (42 g)

¼ cup (28 g) ground cumin
3 tablespoons (4 g) dried parsley
2¼ teaspoons garlic powder
1 teaspoon ground coriander
1 teaspoon dried oregano
1 teaspoon sea salt
1 teaspoon sesame seeds

½ teaspoon dried crushed rosemary
½ teaspoon ground turmeric
¼ teaspoon ground cinnamon
⅛ teaspoon ground ginger
⅛ teaspoon ground cloves
⅛ teaspoon cayenne pepper

Mix all of the spices and store in an airtight container.

Chai Spice Blend

I like to call this blend the exotic cousin of pumpkin pie seasoning. It has the familiar warmness of baking spices with an added twist from the pepper, cardamom, and coriander. It actually pairs so well with pumpkin desserts, I may never go back to pumpkin pie seasoning again!

Makes about ⅓ cup (21 g)

3 tablespoons (21 g) ground cinnamon
½ tablespoon ground cloves
1 tablespoon (6 g) ground cardamom
1 tablespoon (6 g) ground ginger

½ teaspoons ground coriander
½ teaspoon white pepper
¼ teaspoon salt

Mix all of the spices and store in an airtight container.

Acknowledgments

Thank you, talented people at Harvard Common Press and Quarto for, once again, turning my recipes and photos into a beautiful work of art. Thank you for giving me another opportunity to do what I love!

To the army of recipe testers who helped me refine and perfect all of the recipes in this book— I could not have done this without you! Thank you so, so much for your feedback. It means more than you know.

My dear Perry's Plate readers. I love knowing that I played a small part in bringing delicious food into your life. Thank you for all of your encouragement, enthusiasm, and sticking around all of these years.

To my friends and family, thank you for accepting my food offerings and for your honest feedback! And for your patience as I struggled to keep all my plates spinning, occasionally dropping a few.

To Steve and our kids—Thank you for supporting me a second time around and for your faith and confidence in my abilities. It means everything to me. And thank you for (mostly) being willing to eat leftovers of the same thing over and over as I refined the recipes in this book and being patient with me as I spent hours on my laptop and in the kitchen. I owe you a vacation.

About the Author

Natalie Perry started her blog, Perry's Plate (perrysplate.com), in 2008. Her website has had a paleo/gluten-free focus since 2012, and now that paleo is mainstream, her loyal readers continue to visit Perry's Plate for creative, big-flavor recipes that don't take forever to make. She is a regular contributor to "Food and Friends" at ThePioneerWoman.com, and her recipes and writing have also appeared in *Bon Appetit*, *Glamour*, and *Clean Eating* magazines, along with Whole30.com, BuzzFeed, Huffington Post, and other websites. She lives in the Reno/Tahoe Nevada area with her husband and four children.

Index